WITHDRAWN

Browning's Essay on Chatterton

LONDON : GEOFFREY CUMBERLEGE
OXFORD UNIVERSITY PRESS

Browning's

ESSAY ON CHATTERTON

EDITED WITH INTRODUCTORY CHAPTERS AND NOTES

By DONALD SMALLEY

WITH A FOREWORD BY
WILLIAM C. DE VANE

HARVARD UNIVERSITY PRESS
CAMBRIDGE, MASSACHUSETTS

· 1948 ·

Foreword

WHEN Browning, in 1837, gave to his friend and defénder, John Forster, the famous copy of *Pauline* which had once been in the possession of John Stuart Mill, he wrote an illuminating note about himself on the fourth page:

The following Poem was written in pursuance of a foolish plan which occupied me mightily for a time, and which had for its object the enabling me to assume & realize I know not how many different characters; — meanwhile the world was never to guess that "Brown, Smith, Jones & Robinson" (as the spelling books have it) the respective authors of this poem, the other novel, such an opera, such a speech, etc. etc. were no other than one and the same individual. The present abortion was the first work of the Poet *of the batch, who would have been more legitimately* myself *than most of the others; but I surrounded him with all manner of (to my then notion) poetical accessories, and had planned quite a delightful life for him.*

Only this crab remains of the shapely Tree of Life in this Fool's paradise of mine. — R. B.

So far no novel, opera, or speech by Browning has come to light, but it is by no means impossible that such things exist. The young poet did not give up his ambitions or his anonymity so easily, and a diligent search may add to our knowledge of his many activities in the years of his restless youth before his marriage. A comparable discovery of Browning material is here presented by Professor Donald Smalley, and he should have all the rights and honors of treasure trove. Seldom do such discoveries come by pure chance; they come to those who through their long study, intelligence, and imagination are ready to receive them. Because of his intimate knowledge of Browning's biography and poetry, Professor Smalley knew where to look and what to expect. All scholars and readers of Browning and Chatterton owe him a debt of gratitude. When they read his commentary upon Browning's Essay on Chatterton, they will add to the gratitude a great deal of admiration for the fullness of his learning and the keenness of his analysis. For the student of Browning this is a very important book indeed.

It is not likely, I suppose, that Professor Smalley realized in the first flush of his pleasure at discovering Browning's Essay on Chatterton the full implications of the essay for the development of the nineteenth-century poet. Browning had not mentioned Chatterton frequently in his poetry or in his letters. But Professor Smalley, like an experienced miner, knows that where gold is found there may be a vein to be worked. He has worked the vein in the pages that follow to a most profitable result. Under his keen and imaginative analysis the Essay on Chatterton proves to be precisely the point in Browning's poetic career when he formulated his method of special pleading. In making a case for Chatterton, the impostor, Browning lays bare in prose the method he is to follow in poetry the rest of his life. The essay therefore lets in a flood of light upon Browning's temperament and mind, as well as his peculiar technique as a poet, and illuminates Browning's treatment of his many impostors and dubious characters from 1842 to the end of his life. As Professor Smalley shows us, we see in the Essay on Chatterton

Browning in the act of drawing the plans of the dramatic monologue, his chief contribution to the history of poetic form. Did the Essay show too intimately Browning's workshop for him to acknowledge it?

Through Professor Smalley's insight, moreover, we see confirmed another matter that has heretofore been believed by a few. The idea that Browning possessed a unique "power of psychological dissection," or that his work is "a *vade-mecum* of psychiatric and spiritual guidance," for those who suffer in our bad world, is shown to be an entirely misguided estimate of the poet's powers. The truth is that Browning was incapable of reading history or penetrating the secret of historical characters. This is a harsh judgment, but a true one. The reason for it is very clear, however; it is that Browning was by temperament a hot partisan, and came to every cause with a mind already set in a pattern which made him pre-judge every case from intensely personal predilections. As Professor Smalley wisely says, Browning could only dissect what he had first created. Few will deny the poet an amazing ingenuity in making a case once his point of view has been taken. The effect of this judgment is to disqualify Browning as a historian; it does not lessen his stature as a poet.

But this delay on the threshold is long enough. This is Professor Smalley's book, not mine, and the case he presents here in fullness, clarity, and wisdom stands upon its own feet.

Truth ever, truth only the excellent!

William C. DeVane

Acknowledgments

I wish to acknowledge my deep obligations to Professor John Robert Moore of Indiana University, who generously gave counsel at all stages of this project, and to Dean DeVane of Yale University and Professor James Buell Munn of Harvard University, who read the book in manuscript and offered further invaluable criticisms and suggestions.

For assistance of various kinds I am grateful to Dr. Donald J. Lloyd of the University of Oberlin, Professor Gordon Norton Ray of the University of Illinois, Professor William O. Raymond of Bishop's University, and Professor Carl J. Weber of Colby College. Dr. Gardner B. Taplin of Indiana University has kindly shared with me the task of reading proof.

I have also to thank for many favors the authorities of the Library of Congress, the Harvard College Library, the Newberry Library, the Indiana University Library, and the University of Chicago Library. Acknowledgment is due the Trustees of the British Museum for microfilm and other photographic material and to F. S. Crofts & Company for permission to quote from Dean DeVane's *A Browning Handbook*. The Trustees of Indiana University have been most generous in granting funds essential to this project.

Finally there is my indebtedness to my wife, whose help neither began nor ended with the index.

Donald Smalley

Contents

PART

I

I

INTRODUCTION

IN the Essay on Chatterton, here for the first time presented as his work, Robert Browning argues the case of a fellow poet against the imputations of biographers. No more ingenious or superficially plausible account of Chatterton's mysterious actions has been written. Viewed simply as one noted poet's interpretation of the experiences of another, the Essay is a work of considerable interest.

But there is more in this work than at first meets the eye. It soberly professes to be a trustworthy study in biography; yet it is not actually biography even in the Carlylean sense of the word. It is in reality a creative work of a curious and hybrid sort, an initial exercise of power in a province of writing that Browning was later to make peculiarly his own. The Essay is Browning's first, tentative experiment in the art of special-pleading. It throws no "new light" on Chatterton's career, as it promises to do, save as a theme for an unorthodox artist; the Chatterton that Browning gives us never walked the streets of Bristol. The Essay does, however, shed authentic light upon the intimate traits of Robert Browning's own nature. It affords fresh insight into the ways of Browning's creative thinking.

More than any other work of Browning's, his unacknowledged prose essay throws light upon the basic problem of *The Ring and the Book*. This statement may require some explaining. During the last seventy-five years, Browning's famous poem has become the nucleus of a vast auxiliary literature. Known, probable, and even remotely possible sources and analogues have been published to the amount of hundreds of pages. The Old Yellow Book — the voluminous collection of seventeenth-century documents from which Browning avowedly fashioned the "Ring" of his poem — has been twice translated and edited. Commentaries and researches upon this work, placed side by side, would go far to fill a five-foot shelf. Central to all this literature is a single problem that can never be completely solved — the relation of Browning's creative imagination to the raw materials with which it worked.

Browning himself chose to give this problem its place of importance by claiming for *The Ring and the Book* not only the virtues of art but also the virtues of history. He declared both in and out of his poem that he had simply brought to life the characters and events of the Old Yellow Book. His function as an artist, he maintained, had been purely to unfold the truth of his materials. Writers have long since shown that Browning, in spite of his professions, considerably altered the factual details of the Old Yellow Book; but the extent to which he changed the spirit of his materials, and the motives which impelled the change, still constitute a live question. It is a question that probes perhaps more deeply than any other into the essential character of the poet.

The Essay on Chatterton offers a new approach to the central problem of *The Ring and the Book*, for through it we are able to study the creative process of Browning's famous poem by means of a parallel. In the Essay, as a quarter of a century later in *The Ring and the Book*, Browning under-

4

took to rescue truth that had long lain obscured and helpless for lack of a proper champion. Browning was so confident of having accomplished his purpose that he concluded the Essay by urging other writers in the cause of historical veracity to use his work as a model.

But the Essay, like *The Ring and the Book*, reveals a strange difference between what Browning firmly believed he was doing and what he actually did. It happens that for the Essay also we are able to compare Browning's raw materials with the product that he made of them. What we obtain from the comparison is a new and clearer picture of the curious process by which fact became something quite other than itself in Browning's ruggedly original and creative mind. Browning worked with the factual materials of Chatterton's life, but unconsciously he shaped them into a plot of his own making. Despite his unquestionably sincere belief that he dealt solely in the truth, the narrative and the hero of his prose essay are as authentically the products of his own imagination as if he had set about writing a frankly original drama. They are, indeed, startlingly close to the plot and the hero of *The Return of the Druses*, a drama which Browning had written two years before the Essay.

How the Essay parallels and defines the process of *The Ring and the Book*, and how the Essay epitomizes Browning's essential method will be seen at length in the chapters that follow.

The Essay on Chatterton appeared as "Article VIII" in *The Foreign Quarterly Review* for July, 1842. Like other contributions to this periodical, it was published as a lengthy review rather than an independent study, and it was published anonymously. What seems ample external evidence of Browning's authorship is given in the remainder of this chapter. Internal evidence runs strongly throughout the three chapters following, though matters of broader import make the main current in them. The hardest skeptic will perhaps have his doubts satisfied by the time he has finished the second chapter; but if not, the third should convince him. He will have gained considerably more in the process of conviction, it is hoped, than he could have gained from tables of verbal parallels and word frequencies.

The Essay on Chatterton was recorded as Browning's work a half-century ago in the diary of two Victorian poetesses. Selections from their diary appeared posthumously in 1933,[1] but to my knowledge the importance of the entry of June 1, 1895, there included, has until now escaped comment. Twelve years before the date of this entry, Katherine Bradley and her niece Edith Cooper had begun an exchange of letters with Browning. He soon shared the secret that "Michael Field," the name affixed to *Callirhoë* and other poems of some celebrity, was their common pseudonym. On June 13, 1885, they met Browning for the first time, and after lunch on that day he talked with them "of Chatterton (for whom he has a strange admiration) and Shelley." [2]

During the next four years they enjoyed frequent visits to the home of Browning and his sister Sarianna. An intimate friendship developed between the two women and "the Old," as they habitually call Browning in their journal. His death in 1889 dealt them a heavy blow. They were able, however,

[1] *Works and Days: From the Journal of Michael Field*, edited by T. and D. C. Sturge Moore (London, 1933).

[2] *Works and Days*, p. 11.

to set down in their diary their "flashes of impression" at the burial service in Westminster Abbey, and they added interesting minutiae gleaned from conversations with other of his friends. They kept up a correspondence with Sarianna Browning.

In the spring of 1895 they made a pilgrimage to the "delicious Asolo" of *Pippa Passes*, above Venice, for a fortnight's visit at the home of Sarianna and Browning's son "Pen" (Robert Wiedemann Barrett Browning). At lunch on their twelfth day at Asolo, Sarianna showed them "heaps and heaps of letters" and other "curious things of Robert's," including "his copy of Shelley as a boy — the proof sheets of *Paracelsus*, inscribed to his mother, etc." [3] That afternoon it rained. They all felt "awfully dull." The visitors faithfully wrote in their journal, however, and Edith Cooper recorded: "Now I am going to read 'the Old's' article on *Tasso and Chatterton* in the *Foreign Quarterly Review* for July 1842." [4]

The notation of the periodical, month, and year suggests that Edith realized that the article was not generally known as Browning's, but apparently she found no great interest in it. One gathers that on the rainy afternoon of June 1, 1895, she was scarcely up to the task of reading the article intelligently, for the same paragraph speaks of "Rain — heavy sky — a longing of soul and body for sleep" and, expressively, "Sleep — sleep . . . ." In any event, aside from the publication of the entry in 1933, the matter seems to have been allowed to rest from that day to this.

It was characteristic of Browning that he let the Essay on Chatterton lie neglected during his lifetime, for he seems to

[3] *Works and Days*, p. 207.
[4] *Works and Days*, p. 208.

have placed little value on his abilities in prose. The *Essay on Shelley*, his only acknowledged prose work of any length or importance, might have suffered a similar neglect, except for the good offices of his friends. Elizabeth reported that he made "very light" of it.[5] Browning called it a "little thing . . . not admitting of much workmanship of any kind, if I had it to give." [6] Though the volume of supposed Shelley letters for which it was written as a preface in 1851 was found to be spurious and was suppressed, Browning never included the *Essay on Shelley* in his published works, and apparently made no effort to see that it reached the public before Dr. F. J. Furnivall secured his permission to print it in the Browning Society's papers in 1881.

Sarianna Browning was in all likelihood Edith Cooper's authority for assigning the Essay on Chatterton to Browning. It may well have figured among the "curious things of Robert's" which the poet's sister had revealed to her guests at lunch, along with the proof sheets of *Paracelsus*. Conceivably, "Pen" could have been the immediate authority, but in that event he would be repeating the words of his aunt, or of his father, or of both. Sarianna was the oracle of the household upon matters pertaining to the work of her brother. Her claims to this post, especially in regard to Browning's early career, were incontestable. Up to the time of Browning's marriage in 1846, the family circle, composed of the poet, his parents, and Sarianna, had been intimate and rarely broken. Sarianna's "wonderful memory" is a major source of Browning biography.

[5] *The Letters of Elizabeth Barrett Browning*, edited by Frederic G. Kenyon (New York, 1897), II, 53.

[6] *Letters of Robert Browning, Collected by Thomas J. Wise*, edited by Thurman L. Hood (New Haven, 1933), p. 36.

Over a half-century, then, after publication in a periodical long extinct, the Essay on Chatterton was in the Browning family library at Asolo in Italy.[7] Edith Cooper set it down as Browning's work in the best of all possible places for knowing its authenticity.

Both the periodical in which the Essay was published and the date of publication have special logic, for the July, 1842, issue of *The Foreign Quarterly Review*, as a prefatory notice announces, was the first to appear under a new editor. The new editor was John Forster. Browning's friendship with Forster is a long and often-told story of mutual help and occasional quarrels. Browning profited greatly from the early sponsorship of Forster, who, as chief literary and dramatic critic of the *Examiner*, was a champion worth having. Though there were notable breaks in its continuity, the friendship was an important aspect of Browning's career for many years. In the late months of 1841 and in 1842, the relation was especially cordial. Forster, writing in the *Examiner* for October 2, 1841, was almost alone among reviewers in praising *Pippa Passes*. In December, 1841, Browning, at Forster's request, wrote a stanza to accompany "a divine Venetian work" of the artist Maclise.[8] In issues of the *Examiner* for April 2 and November 26, 1842, Forster lauded *King Victor and King Charles* and *Dramatic Lyrics*, works which received scant at-

---

[7] In May, 1913, the Browning Collections were sold by "Pen" Browning through the London auctioneers Sotheby, Wilkinson, and Hodge. Probably the July, 1842, issue of *The Foreign Quarterly Review* was lumped with other books and periodicals for one of the tantalizing *etc.'s* that follow a great many entries in the catalogue of the sale.

[8] *Letters of Robert Browning*, ed. Hood, p. 7. Browning's stanza was soon after to form the opening lines of his poem *In a Gondola* (see William C. DeVane, *A Browning Handbook*, New York, 1935, pp. 103–104).

tention in other quarters. It was in 1842 that Browning gave Forster the manuscript of *Paracelsus* with an inscription expressing "true thanks for his generous and seasonable public Confession of Faith in me." [9]

Forster seems to have counted upon his friends for the success of his first issue of *The Foreign Quarterly Review*. In a letter of December, 1841, Carlyle wrote Forster that he "dare not promise anything as to the *F. Quarterly* at present." [10] *Cromwell* was demanding all his attention. Edward Bulwer, however, fresh from his study of the French Revolution for *Zanoni*, furnished an article upon the Reign of Terror.[11] Walter Savage Landor contributed an ambitious study of the writings of Catullus for Forster's first issue, and another upon Theocritus for the second.[12] Knowing Browning's command of Italian and his interest in Italian literature, it was natural that Forster should call upon him for an article dealing with the biography of Tasso. It was natural, too, that Browning, who later confessed to having an undue fondness for "morbid cases of the soul," [13] should dispose of Tasso in six paragraphs and turn his talents to making a case for Chatterton along lines characteristic of the dramatic monologues. Once he had found his subject, Browning worked rapidly. His entire apology for Chatterton's career was probably written within the

[9] Richard Renton, *John Forster and His Friendships* (London, 1912), facsimile opposite page 266. The proof sheets of *Paracelsus*, not the manuscript, were later at Asolo.

[10] *New Letters of Thomas Carlyle*, edited by A. Carlyle (London, 1904), I, 242.

[11] Victor A. G. R. Bulwer-Lytton, *The Life of Edward Bulwer, First Lord of Lytton* (London, 1913), II, 51–52.

[12] John Forster, *Walter Savage Landor, a Biography* (London, 1876), p. 435. Forster comments: "These essays, as well as a later one on Petrarch, were written for a review at my request . . . "

[13] *Robert Browning and Julia Wedgwood*, edited by Richard Curle (New York, 1937), p. 143.

five weeks preceding July 1, 1842, the date on which the July *Foreign Quarterly* was published.[14]

Chatterton is mentioned but once in the poetry of Browning — in *Waring*, the whimsical piece which Browning addressed to his friend Alfred Domett.

> *Some Chatterton shall have the luck*
> *Of calling Rowley into life!*   (195–196)[15]

Waring was probably written, Dean DeVane concludes, "in the early summer of 1842." [16] It was written, then, within a few weeks of the publication of the Essay of Chatterton.

---

[14] See note 1 to the text of the Essay.

[15] Except where another edition is cited by name, line numbers beneath quotations from Browning's poems and dramas refer to *The Works of Robert Browning* (*Centenary Edition*), 10 vols., edited with introductions by F. G. Kenyon (London, 1912).

[16] *Handbook*, p. 107. Browning also mentions Chatterton in a letter to Domett, November 23, 1845 (*Robert Browning and Alfred Domett*, edited by Frederic G. Kenyon, London, 1906, p. 117), and in the *Essay on Shelley* (*An Essay on Percy Bysshe Shelley*, an edition prepared for the Shelley Society by W. Tyas Harden, London, 1888, p. 24).

II

THE ESSAY AND *THE RING AND THE BOOK*

THE Essay on Chatterton bears witness to the indomitable originality of its author. Browning wrote it as a study in criticism and biography for a sober quarterly review. His stated purpose was to correct the mistakes of earlier biographers, and to "throw a new light" upon Chatterton's character through an intensive reëxamination of the facts of his career. Browning tried to assume a judicious tone; he gave much attention to the details of his sources; he even resorted to the use of footnotes in order to reinforce his arguments. Yet in spite of himself, and all unwittingly, he wrote as a creative artist. He worked with the details of Chatterton's life, but from them he evolved the action and the protagonist of a drama. He sincerely attempted to arrive at a plainer view of Chatterton than biographers had achieved, and he ended by producing a remarkable example of ingenious plotting, special-pleading, and case-making.

As intimated in the first chapter, this central paradox of the Essay is also the paradox of *The Ring and the Book*. The purpose of the present chapter is to show how Browning's unacknowledged prose work of 1842 parallels and anticipates his famous poem.

The Essay and "The Ring and the Book"

I

It has long been recognized that *The Ring and the Book* offers a rare opportunity for following the hand of a poet in his work. At every turn of the poem it is possible to compare the finished product with the raw materials which the author had at his disposal. By tracing the relation of Browning's handiwork to the Old Yellow Book — the golden "Ring" to the "crude fact" from which he avowedly fashioned it — we obtain insight into the author's habits of mind that could hardly be gained in any other way. We secure, as Dean DeVane has said, "a knowledge of the essential Browning":

From . . . detailed analysis of Browning's indebtedness in each part of his great poem, we rise to the larger question of the poet's fidelity to the spirit of the Old Yellow Book. How far did he give truth and truth only as he found it in his source? How far tenable is his own contention (I, 686–7) that he merely resuscitated, rather than created, the personages of his drama? How far has his imagination, which he calls "Fancy," wrung the fact of the murder-case to fit a preconceived view? How far has the alloy given form and color to the golden ring, and how much alloy remains in the finished poem? This question in its many ramifications has troubled scholars since the poem appeared, and it is a question worthy of debate, for through it we attain a knowledge of the essential Browning.[1]

The Browning that we see by comparing the "Book" with the "Ring" worked as an original and strong-minded poet. He recast the facts of the Old Yellow Book to fit a largely

---

[1] *A Browning Handbook*, p. 299.

13

subjective and preconceived view of the case. By bent and habit a dramatic poet, he used the records of the Roman murder-case as the basis for intense and meaningful drama. He changed the merely pathetic individuals who figure in the pleadings and counter-pleadings of the trial into the dramatis personae of a tragedy.

The intellectual villain of *The Ring and the Book*, the heroine impelled by virtue and maternal love, the latter-day Saint George who rescues her, are Browning's improvements upon nature. In the Old Yellow Book, Guido is "merely a weak and avaricious man, vicious by force of circumstances as well as from inherent defects of character." [2] In the poem he becomes a formidable creature, Iago-like in cunning and maleficence. The Pompilia of the Old Yellow Book is "an ordinary girl, deprived of advantages in childhood, with sufficient good looks to attract, and insufficient character to resist temptation." Desperate in her unfortunate marriage, driven by "instincts stronger than her principles," she is pathetic but scarcely admirable. Browning transformed her into a moving symbol of high-mindedness and self-sacrifice. The Caponsacchi of the documents is "a frivolous young fellow . . . light in thought and unscrupulous in action." Browning quite unhistorically regenerates him. Through the need and the influence of Pompilia, the gay young canon of Arezzo turns militant Christian, a rescuing soldier-saint.

But *The Ring and the Book* is by no means simply a romantic fantasy upon an historic theme. It is permeated with a realism which, John Morley testified early in 1869, had

[2] Quotations in this paragraph are from John Marshall Gest's *The Old Yellow Book . . . A New Translation with Explanatory Notes and Critical Chapters upon the Poem and Its Source* (Boston, 1925), pp. 624–625.

struck Victorian drawing-rooms like a "rude inburst of air from the outside welter of human realities." [3] The realism of the poem is the realism of its source. The factual detail of the Old Yellow Book is forced to argue against itself, to give substance and the semblance of reality to the characters of a drama. The process is not uncommon nor of itself necessarily effective, but in Browning's hands it became an instrument of surpassing power. Such was his peculiar cast of mind that he could employ this process with the perfect confidence and sureness of touch of one who dealt solely in the unleavened bread of truth.

Browning sincerely believed that he was portraying the unadulterated fact of the Old Yellow Book. He took

infinite pains . . . to arrive at the truth. He read the Old Yellow Book eight times; he searched in Rome for more materials; he travelled to Arezzo. . . . What a tremendous effort the poet made to transcribe the truth of small details from his sources can only be appreciated by one who has read the Old Yellow Book almost as often as did Browning.[4]

He gave much of the first book of his poem to an elaborate profession of his fidelity to history while pursuing art. His function as an artist, Browning held, had been simply the enabling fact to speak for itself. His imagination had served only as a goldsmith's alloy which renders the pure gold tractable to hammer and file. Once the Ring was fashioned and the alloy removed, the truth of the Old Yellow Book, pristine in purity despite intermediate tempering and shaping, remained:

[3] "On 'The Ring and the Book,' " *The Fortnightly Review*, XI (1869), 331.
[4] DeVane, *Handbook*, p. 299.

> *such alloy,*
> *Such substance of me interfused the gold*
> *Which, wrought into a shapely ring therewith,*
> *Hammered and filed, fingered and favoured, last*
> *Lay ready for the renovating wash*
> *O' the water. "How much of the tale was true?"*
> *I disappeared; the book grew all in all;*
> *The lawyers' pleadings swelled back to their size —*
> *Doubled in two, the crease upon them yet,*
> *For more commodity of carriage, see! —*
> *And these are letters, veritable sheets*
> *That brought posthaste the news to Florence, . . .*
>
> (I, 681–692)

Browning was willing to drop the metaphor and insist upon his method in plain prose. Two days before the first volume of his poem was given to the public, he wrote Julia Wedgwood that his business had been purely and solely "to explain *fact*":

> *and the fact is what you see and, worse, are to see. . . . Before I die, I hope to purely invent something, — here my pride was concerned to invent nothing: the minutest circumstance that denotes character is* true: *the black is so much — the white, no more. You are quite justified perhaps in saying "Let all that black alone" — but, touching it at all, so much of it must be.*[5]

After the publication of his poem Browning went on maintaining that he had merely brought the Old Yellow Book to life. He insisted, according to the Rev. John W. Chadwick,

---

[5] *Robert Browning and Julia Wedgwood*, p. 144.

that he had found Pompilia in his source "just as she speaks and acts in my poem." [6]

Browning was confident that, far from warping fact to fit a plan and characters of his own, he had given an immeasurably clearer view of the truth than the pleadings and counter-pleadings, the pamphlets and the letters of his source could offer unaided:

> *Was this truth of force?*
> *Able to take its own part as truth should,*
> *Sufficient, self-sustaining? Why, if so —*
> *Yonder's a fire, into it goes my book,*
> *As who shall say me nay, and what the loss?*
>
> (I, 372–376)

The lawyers of the Roman murder-case had merely confused issues, missing entirely the subtler import of the evidence:

> *Then, since a Trial ensued, a touch o' the same*
> *To sober us, flustered with frothy talk,*
> *And teach our common sense its helplessness.*
> *For why deal simply with divining-rod,*
> *Scrape where we fancy secret sources flow,*
> *And ignore law, the recognized machine,*
> *Elaborate display of pipe and wheel*
> *Framed to unchoke, pump up and pour apace*
> *Truth till a flowery foam shall wash the world?*
> *The patent truth-extracting process, — ha?*
>
> (I, 1105–1114)

The motives which impelled Pompilia and Caponsacchi had been grossly maligned, Browning felt, by law's coarse and

---

[6] George Willis Cooke, *A Guide-Book to the Poetic and Dramatic Works of Robert Browning* (Boston, 1891), p. 337.

confident process. The truth of the flight from Arezzo, a revelation of altruistic courage and selfless love, had lain in the Old Yellow Book obscure and ineffective until Robert Browning, prober of hidden motive and analyst of souls, had appeared to rescue it.

2

A quarter of a century earlier, Browning had made it his business to explain fact in another instance where truth cried out for a champion. Here also Browning's scorn for the results accomplished by professional sifters of truth and searchers of motive is an important factor. As the lawyers had misunderstood the lofty impulsions which guided Pompilia and Caponsacchi, so biographers had failed utterly to comprehend the high motives which underlay the facts of Chatterton's career. It was to "throw a new light" upon the data of the biographers and thus rescue a reputation which had been "foully outraged" that Browning undertook the Essay.

In the biographies of Chatterton, as in the pamphlets and letters of the Old Yellow Book, Browning found a mass of factual material where truth lay awaiting the authentic analyst of human motive. We can again trace the course of his hand in reshaping his material to his own view of the truth. A comparison of the Essay with its sources shows that in the prose work of 1842 Browning worked in essentially the same manner as in shaping *The Ring and the Book*. Into the biographical data Browning read a thoroughly unhistorical revelation of spiritual redemption and courageous conflict with the forces of darkness. He evolved from Chatterton's pathetic story of moody pride, frustration, and suicide the plan and the protagonist of an edifying moral drama. As in the poem

18

published twenty-six years later, Browning worked by forcing factual detail to argue against itself, to give substance and
plausibility to a plot and a hero of his own invention. The
Chatterton of the Essay is as distinctly a product of Browning's creative imagination as is the Pompilia of *The Ring and
the Book*.

Browning's conviction that his power to create dramatic
character and situation was instead a power to extract objective
truth from his materials could hardly have carried him further
or have revealed itself more clearly. Even his assurances to
Julia Wedgwood that he had invented nothing in *The Ring
and the Book* scarcely parallel his presenting the Essay in a
sober quarterly review as a factual study that proposed to
correct the mistakes of Chatterton's biographers.

3

In the Essay on Chatterton as in *The Ring and the Book*,
Browning dealt with a body of evidence that had already
been argued from widely divergent points of view. The
exact motives that guided Chatterton in his brief but colorful
career are still a subject of debate and are likely to remain so.

Thomas Chatterton was born on November 20, 1752, the
posthumous son of a writing-master and lay clerk of Bristol
Cathedral. After attending Colston's School, a charity institution where only writing and accounts were taught, he was
apprenticed on July 1, 1767, at the age of fourteen, to John
Lambert, a Bristol attorney. Even while at Colston's he had
written a satire entitled "Apostate Will" (1764) and other
verses. In 1768, upon the opening of a new bridge at Bristol,
an account of the ceremony that accompanied the opening
of the old bridge in the thirteenth century was published in

Felix Farley's Bristol Journal. This account was in archaic language, and a note to the printer signed "Dunhelmus Bristoliensis" stated that the narrative was "taken from an old manuscript." Excited citizens traced the document to Chatterton, who at first refused to give any explanation. After threats and promises had been directed at him, however, he asserted that the original was one of many ancient manuscripts which had belonged to his father, who had taken them from a large chest in the muniment room of Redcliffe Church.

For William Barrett, a surgeon then engaged in writing a history of Bristol, and for George Catcott, pewterer, Chatterton fabricated archaic documents and poems of which he claimed to possess the originals. In a few instances he produced "originals" by a clever imitation of antique writing on ancient parchment or on parchment made to appear antique through the use of various materials including ocher and black lead powder. Chief among his gifts to his patrons were the poems and prose writings of Thomas Rowley, a fifteenth-century Bristol monk wholly of Chatterton's creation, who gratefully acknowledged the munificent patronage of William Canynge, an historical Bristol merchant. Chatterton's own patrons were far from liberal, and his apprenticeship to Lambert seems to have been anything but pleasant to him. He tried to interest Dodsley, the London publisher, in Rowley's poetry. Failing in this, he approached Horace Walpole, sending the author of *Anecdotes of Painting in England* transcripts of Rowley's prose dissertations on the history of art. Though at first deceived, Walpole declined Chatterton's suit for patronage.

In April, 1770, Chatterton left Bristol for London. After four months spent in vainly attempting to make a living by contributions to the periodicals and the writing of a burletta, he took his life by means of poison [7] (August 24, 1770) at the age of seventeen.

Chatterton wrote so successfully in the archaic vein that for decades after his death the question whether an actual fifteenth-century monk named Thomas Rowley had written the pieces attributed to him remained a live issue. For Jacob Bryant [8] and Jeremiah Milles,[9] chief supporters of Rowley, an explanation of Chatterton's motives was comparatively simple. He was an idle attorney's clerk who attempted to capitalize upon his possession of antique manuscripts by releasing transcripts of them to his patrons. Though he was a youth of some parts, he was incapable of writing the Rowley poems. They were quite willing to agree with Mrs. Newton's assertion in her letter to Sir Herbert Croft that her brother had been "a lover of truth from the earliest dawn of reason." [10]

Writers who accepted Chatterton as the creator of Rowley, however, were far from agreed upon his character and motives. Was he essentially an innocent poet-soul who lived apart dreaming of former ages, and who perished in his youth because of the world's neglect? Or was he essentially a precocious impostor with a deep-rooted love of making older

---

[7] Unless he killed himself unintentionally, as appears unlikely, by taking an overdose of a medicine for venereal disease. See E. H. W. Meyerstein's articles, "Thomas Chatterton," [London] *Times Literary Supplement*, June 25, 1931, p. 504, and "Chatterton's Last Days," *ibid.*, June 28, 1941, p. 316.

[8] *Observations upon the Poems of Thomas Rowley, in which the Authenticity of those Poems is Ascertained* (London, 1781).

[9] *Poems Supposed to Have Been Written at Bristol in the Fifteenth Century by Thomas Rowley . . . with a Commentary by Jeremiah Milles, D. D., Dean of Exeter* (London, 1782).

[10] See note 12 to the text of the Essay.

men his dupes, a writer of scurrilous and sometimes unprint-able satires, who boasted his atheistic principles and died by his own hand, impenitent? Both extreme views and numerous gradations between them have appeared in print. The tradi-tion of an otherworldly Chatterton, killed by society's indif-ference to poets, has persisted to the present day, though its chief nourishment has always been sentiment rather than fact. Even from the start, biographers found it necessary to recog-nize that however much Chatterton lived with Rowley, he knew somewhat more than enough of the life of contemporary Bristol.

Sir Herbert Croft, the first biographer of Chatterton worthy of the name, had no inclination either to censure or to con-done the Rowley impostures. He was willing to accept Chat-terton as an inexplicable genius without bothering greatly about the moral attributes of his character: "Most readily I admit that, if Chatterton be an impostor (i. e. the wonderful human being I firmly believe him), he imposed upon every soul who knew him. This with me, is one trait of his great-ness." [11]

Dr. George Gregory, writing in 1789, took a sterner view. In his eyes, Chatterton was a wild youth who, because of reckless misuse of his genius and the adoption of unsound principles, came to a bad end that might serve as an object lesson to later generations:

The whole of Chatterton's life presents a fund of useful instruction to young persons of brilliant and lively talents, and affords a strong dissuasive against that impetuosity of ex-

[11] *Love and Madness. A Story Too True* (London, 1780), p. 140. I quote from the first of the four editions of 1780. *Love and Madness* is a curious novel purportedly giving the love letters of Martha Ray and the Reverend James Hack-

pectation, and those delusive hopes of success, founded upon the consciousness of genius and merit, which lead them to neglect the ordinary means of acquiring competence and independence. The early disgust which Chatterton conceived for his profession, may be accounted one of the prime sources of his misfortunes.[12]

When in 1803 Robert Southey and Joseph Cottle edited the first collection of Chatterton's works pretending to completeness, they were content to republish Dr. Gregory's *Life* with but little additional commentary. Though the edition was intended as a tribute to Chatterton's memory, the profits from it going toward the support of his mother and sister, the editors felt no impulsion to soften Dr. Gregory's judgment. On the contrary, Cottle gave imposture as the very key to Chatterton's character:

Whoever closely examines the Life and Writings of Chatterton, will remark that he seemed to be strikingly influenced by one particular disposition of mind, and that was, through an excess of ingenuity, in a literary sense, to impose on the credulity of others. This predominant quality elucidates his character, and is deserving of minute regard by all who attempt to decide on the Rowleian controversy.[13]

Even before Croft wrote, however, Chatterton had touched the public fancy as the Neglected Genius. Croft himself,

---

man, who was hanged at Tyburn in April, 1779, as her murderer. Letter XLIX (pp. 125–244) is a vivid account of Chatterton's life and poetry, still a major source for Chatterton biography.

[12] *The Life of Thomas Chatterton, with Criticisms on his Writings* (London, 1789), pp. 37–38.

[13] "Observations on Chatterton's Arms," *The Works of Thomas Chatterton* (London, 1803), II, 509.

while freely admitting and detailing Chatterton's peccadilloes, had felt the attractions of this view. He had forbidden age and pharisaic morality the right "to attack this infant Hercules in his cradle." [14] In 1782 an engraving entitled "The Distressed Poet," depicting an impoverished Chatterton writing in his London garret, was published in the *Westminster Magazine*, and shortly afterward the same picture, slightly altered, was printed in red and blue upon The Chatterton Handkerchief with suitable legend and verses. "Anxieties and cares," the legend tells us,

had advanced his life, and given him an older look than was suited to his age. . . Hard indeed was his fate, born to adorn the times in which he lived, yet compelled to fall a victim to pride and poverty! His destiny, cruel as it was, gives a charm to his verses, and while the bright thought excites admiration, the recollection of his miseries awakens a tender sympathy and sorrow.[15]

Indignation as well as sympathy and sorrow had been awakened. Walpole had judged it expedient in 1779 to publish an elaborate defense against charges of responsibility for Chatterton's distress through his refusal of patronage to the transcriber of Rowley.[16]

The Romantic poets found in Chatterton a moving symbol of their plight within a world absorbed in getting and spending. Coleridge's youthful tribute to "free Nature's genial child" [17] (1794) was printed after Dr. Gregory's *Life* in

[14] *Love and Madness*, p. 133.
[15] See E. H. W. Meyerstein, *A Life of Thomas Chatterton* (London, 1930), illustration opposite p. 476.
[16] See note 38 to the text of the Essay.
[17] "Monody on the Death of Chatterton," line 66.

Southey and Cottle's edition of Chatterton's works, where it makes curious reading beside the austere biographer's analysis. Wordsworth, in momentary dejection, thought

> *of Chatterton, the marvellous Boy,*
> *The sleepless Soul that perished in his pride;*
>
> .　.　.　.　.
>
> *We poets in our youth begin in gladness;*
> *But thereof come in the end despondency and madness.*[18]

Keats inscribed *Endymion* (1818) to the memory of Chatterton. Shelley enthroned the boy-poet among the "inheritors of unfulfilled renown":

> *Chatterton*
> *Rose pale, — his solemn agony had not*
> *Yet faded from him;*[19]

Alfred de Vigny in his drama *Chatterton* (1835) put blood into an anemic symbol, for the hero of Vigny's tragedy is a vigorous character, though greatness of spirit renders him incapable of surviving in the petty competitions of a petty world. But Vigny's Chatterton draws most of his vitality from the French poet who begot him. He is most convincing when he is farthest from Mrs. Angel's garret in Brook Street, Holborn.

While the tradition of a Chatterton too noble for the world's possessing throve among poets and prose rhapsodists, biographers continued to draw a less engaging portrait. John Davis's *The Life of Thomas Chatterton* (1806) is merely a hack's garbling of Croft and Gregory, scarcely attaining a

---

[18] *Resolution and Independence* (1807), ll. 43–49.
[19] *Adonais* (1821), ll. 399–401.

point of view of its own, but Alexander Chalmers in 1810 outdid Dr. Gregory in moral censure upon Chatterton's life, "every part of which proves his utter contempt for truth at an age when we are taught to expect a disposition open, ingenuous, and candid." [20]

Two lives of Chatterton appeared early in the Victorian period, and it was primarily against these works as the latest outrages against Chatterton's memory that Browning directed his Essay. Both play uncritically upon the pathos of Chatterton's career, but both are specific upon his activities as a cozener of his elders and a satirist wise beyond his years in knowledge less innocent than that which went into the writings of Rowley. John Dix, the earlier of the two, published in 1837 [21] a considerable amount of new material, though a portion of it is far from trustworthy.[22] Dix agrees with Joseph Cottle that imposture is the key to Chatterton's character; like Croft, he accepts Chatterton's success in his deceptions as a trait of his greatness:

It has been observed, that the pedigree of De Bergham forms a subject for important consideration, exhibiting an unquestionable proof of that radical *tendency of mind which Chatterton felt for inventing plausible fictions, and in support of which sentiment his whole life forms one mass of authority. Few can doubt but that Chatterton possessed that peculiar dis-*

---

[20] "The Life of Thomas Chatterton," *The Works of the English Poets,* edited by Alexander Chalmers (London, 1810), XV, 378.

[21] *The Life of Thomas Chatterton, Including His Unpublished Poems and Correspondence* (London, 1837).

[22] See Meyerstein, *Life,* p. xix, and *Notes and Queries,* Fourth Series, ix, 294–296, 365–366, 429–430; x, 55, 229–230. But Dix (*Life,* p. 292) was careful not to vouch for the absurd story of the reinterment of Chatterton's remains at Bristol, presenting it as "purely a matter of speculation."

position, as well as those pre-eminent talents, the union of which was both necessary and equal to the great production of Rowley.[23]

Whereas Gregory and Chalmers had considered Chatterton's impostures a subject for moral censure, Dix admired the ease with which the boy hoodwinked his parsimonious patrons. Chatterton was "pleased with his success" in leading on the "credulous historian," and "the pretended young transcriber smiled, at the dupe of his ingenuity" from behind the cowl of " 'Thomas Rowley, the gode prieste.' "[24] In general, loftier moral ground is taken in the biography which appeared early in 1842 as a lengthy preface to a new edition of Chatterton's works. C. B. Willcox, the anonymous author of the life and editor of the works,[25] felt that if Chatterton's falsifying of history could escape severe censure, it at least required considerable explaining:

> *But a wide difference [exists] between the pseudo-poet and the pretended historian. Heartily, for the fair fame of Thomas Chatterton, is it to be wished that he had never met with Barrett, or that Barrett, as he afterwards did, had offended him at the first outset. . . . But let us be sparing of blame, at least, till we have rightly unravelled the mysteries of his character, and have seen how far the* passion *of imposing upon the credulity of his fellows made up the* LIFE, *the* BEING *(without which he could not* be) *of this extraordinary boy.*[26]

[23] *Life*, p. 24.
[24] Dix, *Life*, pp. 61–62.
[25] *The Poetical Works of Thomas Chatterton with Notices of his Life* (Cambridge, 1842). The two volumes are paged consecutively, the second beginning at page 321.
[26] *Life*, p. lxxii.

Willcox found it "difficult to form a just appreciation of the character of Chatterton"[27] and managed to avoid facing the task directly. Conceding that Chatterton "too often obeyed the suggestions of the evil heart," he nevertheless dared hope that had Chatterton continued among the living, he would in time have reformed.[28]

Since the appearance of the Essay in July, 1842, the debate over Chatterton's motives and character has continued.[29] In 1857 the Rev. S. R. Maitland, last of the Rowleyans, went even beyond Chalmers in blackening the boy-poet. Chatterton, because he was "an unprincipled impostor," a profligate, "an habitual and gross liar," and no great poet in his acknowledged writings, could never have created Rowley.[30] Sir Daniel Wilson in 1869 published his *Chatterton: A Biographical Study*,[31] still a standard biography. Condemning the unwarrantably harsh verdict of Maitland,[32] Wilson painted Chatterton in much lighter colors:

Chatterton's masking began as an innocent dream of the child-poet, and appears to have been cherished by him to the last as an ideal reality. But it inevitably tended to become a deception, with more or less of sheer falsehood, when maintained with the help of spurious manuscripts and fictitious details of the literary treasures purloined from Canynge's coffer. Nevertheless the striking contrast between the trans-

---

[27] *Ibid.*, p. cxlii.

[28] *Life*, pp. cxlv–cxlvi.

[29] To my knowledge, no later biographer of Chatterton has mentioned the Essay. It is not listed in Francis Adams Hyett and the Reverend Canon Bazeley's bibliography *Chattertonia* (Gloucester, 1914).

[30] *Chatterton: An Essay* (London, 1857), pp. 22, 47, *et passim*.

[31] London, 1869.

[32] *Chatterton*, p. xiii.

*parent veil of fiction which his mother and sister were allowed
to look through, and the impenetrable mystery which was opposed to the searching eye of strangers, must not be overlooked
in judging of his conduct in this false position.*[33]

Even in Wilson's sympathetic hands the innocent child-poet
soon turns into the knowing boy who delights in tricking his
seniors. Writing pseudo-antique poetry is one thing; falsifying history by the coining of spurious documents in prose is
another. It was no guileless dreamer who practised upon
Barrett's gullibility: "How the antiquarian dupe must have
gloated over his prizes; while the adept laughed in his sleeve
at the airs assumed by his condescending patron!" [34] Wilson
found it necessary to concede that Chatterton had a darker
side. He wished that *The Exhibition* with its evidence that
"the precocious boy was only too conversant with forbidden
things" had perished.[35] Though he denied that there was evidence of the boy's "systematic profligacy," he granted that
"there are passages in Chatterton's modern prose and verse,
and allusions in his letters, which repel by their irreverence,
and at times by their impurity." [36]

The Chatterton of the Romantic poets has persisted. Henry
Wallis's famous painting of Chatterton's death scene (1856)
inevitably fostered this tradition. In prose it has been kept
alive notably in Charles Edward Russell's *Thomas Chatterton: The Marvellous Boy* [37] and to a lesser extent in John H.
Ingram's *The True Chatterton.*[38] In addition, Chatterton

[33] *Chatterton*, pp. 127–128.
[34] *Ibid.*, p. 120.
[35] *Ibid.*, pp. 200–201.
[36] *Ibid.*, pp. 203–204.
[37] New York, 1908.
[38] London, 1910.

has been psychoanalyzed according to Adlerian theories as a neurotic.[39]

Meyerstein in his invaluable biography (1930) quotes a biographical dictionary of 1784 as an index of his own estimate of Chatterton's character:

This unfortunate person, though certainly a most extraordinary genius, seems yet to have been a most ungracious composition. He was violent and impetuous to a strange degree. From the first of the above-cited letters to his sister [May 30, 1770] he appears to have had a portion of ill-humour and spleen more than enough for a youth of 17.[40]

Meyerstein willingly grants that in part Chatterton was "the romantic child whose day-dreams were peopled by fifteenth century familiars." But

the intense dreariness, the fiery egotism, the abstracted and bitter melancholy, finding most relief in imitative satire, when the garb of the imaginary monk was thrown by, this is the Thomas Chatterton whom Bristol saw, knew, and remembered, a being whom we are permitted to recapture: the other is inherent in the Rowley cycle, it scarcely has an existence outside.[41]

Thus Chatterton remains two personalities. It is doubtful whether future biographers can do better than to recognize this fact.

This brief review has, it is hoped, made evident that Chatterton's career and character offer a subject scarcely less rich

---

[39] Esther Parker Ellinger, *Thomas Chatterton: The Marvelous Boy* (University of Pennsylvania Press, 1930).

[40] *Life*, p. xii.

[41] *Life*, p. xv.

in ambiguous detail and complex motivation than the history of Pompilia and Caponsacchi. It is not surprising that Alfred de Vigny, like Browning, found Chatterton a subject to his hand. But Vigny was content to exert a poet's prerogative, giving his hero new surroundings, new confidants, a Lord Talbot, and a Kitty Bell when biography failed to suit his purposes. No concern for fidelity to history restrained his hand from drawing an ideal Chatterton: "Le Poète était tout pour moi; Chatterton n'était qu'un nom d'homme, et je viens d'écarter à dessein des faits exacts de sa vie pour ne prendre de sa destinée que ce qui la rend un exemple à jamais déplorable d'une noble misère." [42] For Browning, this declaration of freedom from biography would have been unthinkable. The basic fact of the Essay on Chatterton as of *The Ring and the Book*, is that the poet who wrote it was confident that he was working as an historian.

4

Whereas the Romantic poets had enrolled Chatterton in their catalogue of martyr saints without difficulty by simply ignoring the embarrassing details of his life, Browning proposed to exalt Chatterton's memory by a quite different process. It was his intention to meet biographers on their own terms. It will be seen at length in the notes to the present edition of the Essay that he studied the biographies of Chatterton intensively. Though he obviously drew upon the lives of Dix and Willcox for the greater part of his material, he also shows a command of detail in the volumes of Croft,

[42] "Dernière Nuit de Travail," *Chatterton*, edited by Henri Maugis (Paris, 1937), p. 24. For a full account of Vigny's use of Chatterton biography and legend, see C. Wesley Bird's *Alfred de Vigny's Chatterton* (Los Angeles, 1941).

Bryant, Gregory, and Southey and Cottle. As in *The Ring and the Book*, however, Browning mastered the detail of his sources only to warp it to a pattern eminently of his own making. The Chatterton of the Essay is not the attorney's apprentice, knowing in "forbidden things" and adept in duplicity and satire, that Bristol saw; neither is he by any means the pale dreamer of Shelley's kingdom. Like Browning's Caponsacchi, Browning's Chatterton is an idealized character, but idealized in accordance with the muscular ethics of his creator. Losing authenticity, he scarcely loses vigor.

In the Essay, Chatterton is for the first time defended in the courts of evangelical Christianity. He had been condemned in them by Dr. Gregory and Chalmers and, to a lesser extent, by Willcox. Nine years later, in the *Essay on Shelley*, Browning was to argue another poet's case in the same courts. The similarities in his briefs for the two poets are illuminating:

1. *Both had been maligned in biography.*

Chatterton:

He is to the present day viewed as a kind of Psalmanazar or Macpherson, producing deliberately his fabrications to the world and challenging its attention to them. A view far from the truth. (226–229)[43] [Other passages are discussed in the pages following.]

Shelley:

But in this respect was the experience of Shelley peculiarly unfortunate — that the disbelief in him as a man, even pre-

[43] Line numbers in parentheses are used here and throughout the introductory chapters to refer to the present text of the Essay on Chatterton. Numbers in paren-

ceded the disbelief in him as a writer; the misconstruction of
his moral nature preparing the way for the misappreciation
of his intellectual labors. . . A full life of Shelley should be
written at once, while the materials for it continue in reach;
not to minister to the curiosity of the public, but to obliterate
the last stain of that false life which was forced on the public's
attention before it had any curiosity on the matter, — a biog-
raphy, composed in harmony with the present general dis-
position to have faith in him, yet not shrinking from a candid
statement of all ambiguous passages, through a reasonable
confidence that the most doubtful of them will be found con-
sistent with a belief in the eventual perfection of his character,
according to the poor limits of our humanity. (19–20)

2. *Both were geniuses. Genius is essentially moral.*
   Chatterton:

. . . being, as such a genius could not but be, the noblest-
hearted of mortals. (820–821)

Seeing cause for faith in something external and better, and
having attained to a moral end and aim, [genius] next dis-
covers in itself the only remaining antagonist worthy of its
ambition, and in the subduing what at first had seemed its most
enviable powers, arrives at the more or less complete fulfil-
ment of its earthly mission. (187–193)

Shelley:

Certainly, in the face of any conspicuous achievement of
genius, philosophy, no less than sympathetic instinct, warrants

---

theses following quotations from the *Essay on Shelley* refer to the pages of the
edition prepared by W. Tyas Harden for the Shelley Society (London, 1888).

*our belief in a great moral purpose having mainly inspired
even where it does not visibly look out of the same.* (16)

*. . . the whole poet's virtue, I repeat, of looking higher than
any manifestation yet made of both beauty and good . . . to
the present reality of the poet's soul already arrived at the
higher state of development, and still aspirant to elevate and
extend itself in conformity with its still-improving perceptions
of, no longer the eventual Human, but the actual Divine.*
(17–18)

3. *Their early aberrations were merely the pardonable mistakes of boyhood.*

Chatterton:

*Before the world could be appealed to, a few untoward circumstances seem to have effectually determined and given
stability to what else had not impossibly proved a mere boy's
fancy, destined to go as lightly as it came and leave no trace,
save in a fresh exertion of the old means to a new and more
commensurate end.* (230–235)

Shelley:

*Nor will men persist in confounding, any more than God
confounds, with genuine infidelity and an atheism of the heart,
those passionate, impatient struggles of a boy towards distant
truth and love, made in the dark, and ended by one sweep of
the natural seas before the full moral sunrise could shine out
on him. Crude convictions of boyhood, conveyed in imperfect
and inapt forms of speech, — for such things all boys have
been pardoned.* (20)

4. *Only their genius led them into youthful indiscretions which the world took seriously. Mediocre youth is safe from such errors.*

Chatterton:

To the falsehood of the mediocre, truth may easily be super-induced, and true works, with them, silently take the place of false works: but before one like Chatterton could extricate himself from the worse than St. Anna dungeon which every hour was building up more surely between him and the common earth and skies, so much was to be dared and done! (216–222)

This first instinct of Imitation, which with the mediocre takes the corresponding mediocre form of an implied rather than expressed appropriation of some other man's products, assumed perforce with Chatterton, whose capabilities were of the highest class, a proportionably bolder and broader shape in the direction his genius had chosen to take. And this consideration should have checked the too severe judgment of what followed. (193–200)

Shelley:

An ordinary youth, who turns his attention to similar subjects, discovers falsities, incongruities, and various points for amendment, and . . . keeps up before his young eyes so many instances of the same error and wrong, that he finds himself unawares arrived at the startling conclusion, that all must be changed — or nothing: in the face of which plainly impossible achievement, he is apt . . . to refer the whole task to another age and person — safe in proportion to his incapacity. Wanting words to speak, he has never made a fool of

35

himself by speaking. But, in Shelley's case, the early fervour and power to see was accompanied by as precocious a fertility to contrive: *he endeavoured to realise as he went on idealising . . . till suddenly he stood pledged . . . to an attack upon various great principles . . . playing with blind passion into the hands of his enemies . . . mistaking Churchdom for Christianity, and for marriage, "the sale of love" and the law of sexual oppression.* (22–23)

5. *Their writings show that both Chatterton and Shelley were potentially Christians in outlook.*

Chatterton:

But the pieces on devotional subjects, to which his earlier taste inclined, came so profusely from the "Godlie preeste Rowlie," that Chatterton thinks it advisable, from the time of his discoveries, to forget his paraphrases of Job and Isaiah, and to disclaim for himself a belief in Christianity on every and no occasion at all! (336– 340)

Shelley:

Already he had attained to a profession of "a worship to the Spirit of good within, which requires (before it sends that inspiration forth, which impresses its likeness upon all it creates) devoted and disinterested homage," as Coleridge says, *— and Paul likewise.* (23–24)

6. *Had they lived, both would have entered thoroughly upon the ways of Truth.*

Chatterton:

In a word, poor Chatterton's life was not the Lie it is so universally supposed to have been; nor did he "perish in the pride" of refusing to surrender Falsehood and enter on the ways of Truth. We can show, we think . . . that he had already entered on those ways when he was left, without a helping hand, to sink and starve as he might. And to this single point we shall as far as possible restrict ourselves. (142–149)

Shelley:

Gradually he was learning that the best way of removing abuses is to stand fast by truth. Truth is one, as they are manifold; and innumerable negative effects are produced by the upholding of one positive principle. I shall say what I think, — had Shelley lived he would have finally ranged himself with the Christians. (23)

In his two prose essays, then, the anonymous and the acknowledged, Browning was intent upon viewing a romantic rebel as a prodigal son of evangelism. In the *Essay on Shelley*, however, he was content merely to give points to a future biographer, devoting the major part of his work to general remarks upon poetry and poets. In the Essay on Chatterton, character was his dominant concern, and he confidently proceeded to trace the process of redemption at length in the details of Chatterton's life.

As the last passage quoted from the Essay on Chatterton implies, Browning was thoroughly conscious that in portraying Chatterton as perishing not in pride but in the ways of Truth he was opposing what biographers had "universally supposed." In the passage, Browning clearly alludes to the words of Willcox, whose recently published biography had served him as a point of departure for his defense of Chatter-

37

ton's outraged memory.[44] Willcox, like the biographers before him, had seen anything but a return to truth in Chatterton's suicide:

> *It is not our intention to profane the chamber of death, or to pourtray with unavailing and thankless minuteness, the dark imaginings and mental convulsions of "the sleepless boy that perished in his pride." The fearful retrospect and the gloomy anticipation — the bitter thoughts, inflamed and exasperated by the knowledge of what he might have been, contrasted with the consciousness of what he was — the strong man bowed down by physical suffering . . . the humiliation — the despair — the final madness — the solemn agony, and sublime death of the martyred poet, are not to be coldly delineated in words, but are to be realized by the thinking and sympathetic heart alone.[45]*

Willcox had spoken elsewhere of Chatterton's wilfulness and pride:

> *That [Walpole] should be made accountable for Chatterton's suicide, was one of the maddest and most absurd persecutions ever urged against an individual. The proud boy held on his course "unslacked of motion," for more than a twelvemonth afterwards, manifesting the same passion for imposing upon the credulity of others . . .* [46]

In rejecting this view and attempting to show that Chatterton's career was a process of redemption culminated by a final renunciation of falsehood at the doors of death, Browning in

---

[44] See the text of the Essay, ll. 113ff.

[45] *Life*, p. cxxxix.

[46] *Ibid.*, p. cvii. See also pp. liii, lxxiii, cxxi, cxxxiii, and cxlii.

reality evolved a plot as boldly creative as that of Vigny's frankly unhistorical drama. Browning, also, was a dramatic poet, and in July, 1842, his hand was in excellent practice. Within three years, he had written *Pippa Passes*, *King Victor and King Charles*, *The Return of the Druses*, and *A Blot in the 'Scutcheon*, as well as various short dramatic poems. In March, 1842, *King Victor and King Charles* was published. In November, *Dramatic Lyrics*, including *My Last Duchess* and *Soliloquy of the Spanish Cloister*, was to appear. *The Return of the Druses* was to go on the stalls in January, 1843, and *A Blot in the 'Scutcheon* was to be published and acted on February 11, 1843.[47]

In the details of Chatterton's life, Robert Browning, writer of plays and monologues, saw the elements of a dramatic conflict. Chatterton had not perished in pride, but in the throes of a struggle between the "intellectual" and "moral"[48] parts of his nature, a struggle that had begun with his first deceptions.

As Browning saw his course, Chatterton had at first written his pseudo-antique poetry in a harmless attempt to imitate the poetry of an earlier period, an action no more reprehensible than the efforts of other poets in their early imitative period to copy the matter and style of the accepted authors of their day. With the opening of the New Bridge in 1768, however, Chatterton had tried for an audience, with disastrous results. Feeling instinctively that the world would not allow him a hearing in his own name, he had resorted to a device

---

[47] I follow the dates of composition and publication given in Dean DeVane's *Handbook*.

[48] The words are Browning's. See the Essay, ll. 767–773. Browning also applies the terms to Shelley. See the quotation from the *Essay on Shelley* given under point one of the comparison of the two essays above.

common to young writers by presenting his description of the opening of the Old Bridge as a piece "taken from an old manuscript." But Chatterton had written in his archaic style so effectively that the citizens of Bristol accepted his imitation at face value. Promises of patronage for further antique treasures set him upon his "false course." Blind to the true merit of his writings, his patrons valued them only for their supposed antiquity. Henceforward Chatterton must maintain his first pretense or surrender all:

He could only determine for the future to produce Ellas and Godwyns, and other "beauteous pieces;" wherein "the plot should be clear, the language spirited; and the songs interspersed in it, flowing, poetical, and elegantly simple; the similes judiciously applied; and though written in the reign of Henry VI., not inferior to many of the present age." Had there but been any merit of this kind, palpable even to Bristol Literati, to fall back upon in the first instance, if the true authorship were confessed! But that was otherwise; and so the false course, as we have said, was unforeseeingly entered upon. (368–378)

But Chatterton, whose nature was essentially moral, was tortured by his career of deception. He "made the most gallant and manly effort of which his circumstances allowed to break through the sorry meshes that entangled him." (475–478)

Browning's development of this story of boyish innocence betrayed by circumstance and courageous struggle against the meshes of falsehood is woven to an amazing extent from the details of biography itself. Casual readers of *The Foreign Quarterly Review* must have considered his study not only well-argued but convincing. John Forster surely accepted it as trustworthy, for he would not have wished to begin his editorship by publishing what amounts, with all allowances made for Victorian latitudes in biography, to an unintentional literary hoax.

Even at the outset there are two major objections to the validity of Browning's attempt to improve on the biographers. First, though Chatterton undoubtedly spent a part of his time withdrawn from society dreaming of Rowley, he was also an attorney's apprentice who, as we have seen, showed precocity in more than poetry. His early acquaintance James Thistlethwaite allows the inescapable in admitting that "amongst Chatterton's papers may be found many passages, not only immoral, but bordering upon a libertinism gross and unpardonable." [49] Whether such passages were the result of only "a warmth of imagination," as Thistlethwaite preferred to think, or of a "natural depravity," they show a sophistication that the Essay does not take into account, and they are in evidence before the opening of the New Bridge could tempt Chatterton to enter "unforeseeingly," as Browning would have it, upon a course of deception.[50] The prose description of the "Mayor's first passing over the old bridge" was not written by a guileless boy shyly venturing his first display of poetical powers. Chatterton had published an anonymous satire aimed at a churchwarden of Bristol in the same journal four years earlier! [51]

Second, and more important, there is no real evidence to show that Chatterton at any time greatly regretted his impostures or was much concerned about the moral implications

[49] Willcox, *Life*, p. lix.
[50] See, for example, his letter to his friend Baker (Willcox, *Life*, pp. lvi–lvii).
[51] *Ibid.*, pp. xxxvi–xxxvii.

of his work. Browning might have read in Dix and Willcox that Chatterton's first forgery was a clever device for extracting shillings and amusement from the credulous Bristol pewterer Henry Burgum.[52] Burgum paid Chatterton a crown for an elaborate pedigree tracing his descent from "Simon de Leyncte Lyze, *alias* Senliz," who married "Matilda, daughter of Waltheof, Earl of Northumberland, Northampton, and Huntingdon." In his *Will*, a document on which Browning lays considerable stress, Chatterton expresses himself concerning this deception, but his words are not the words of a penitent:

> *Gods! what would Burgum give to get a name,*
> *And snatch his blundering dialect from shame!*
> *What would he give, to hand his memory down*
> *To time's remotest boundary? — a Crown.*
> *Would you ask more, his swelling face looks blue;*
> *Futurity he rates at two pounds two.*[53]

Though Browning could, biographers could not ignore the fact that Chatterton's letter to Dodsley avoids flatly offering the printer "beauteous pieces . . . written in the reign of Henry VI." It states that they are in the possession of a gentleman who "absolutely denies to give me [a copy] unless I give him a guinea for a consideration." [54]

Profit, fame, a passionate love of poetry and of medieval lore, an extraordinary delight in imposture for its own sake all seem to have impelled the Marvellous Boy in his career.

---

[52] Meyerstein (*Life*, p. 151) rejects the tradition that the Burgum Pedigree was written while Chatterton was at Colston's School.

[53] *Works*, ed. Willcox, p. 623. See also Willcox's *Life*, pp. xli–xliii.

[54] Willcox, *Life*, p. lxxxiv.

His motives are strangely interwoven, and his character defies simple analysis. But "boy" is scarcely the word or the attitude in dealing with Chatterton. Another poet writing anonymously in an earlier review came closer to the mark by treating him as "a most active and powerful mind":

for when we consider the strange ambiguity of Chatterton's character, his attainments under circumstances incalculably disadvantageous, and his wish to disguise them under the name of another; his high spirit of independence, and the ready versatility with which he stooped to the meanest political or literary drudgery; the amiable and interesting affection which he displays towards his family, with a certain looseness of morality which approaches to profligacy, — we cannot but regret that a subject, uniting so strong an alternation of light and shade, had not been sketched by the hand of a master. . .

Alike a forger of style, of MSS., and of drawings, nothing escaped the imitation of a youth, born as it were with the rare talents of executing such multiplied deceptions, and with a temper framed to delight in his success, which it may be hoped is still rarer.[55]

Chatterton had genius and possessed some admirable qualities, including filial affection. But there was beyond question far more earth in him than the Essay allows for.

Browning's main point, however, is still to consider. In April, 1770, Chatterton left Bristol for London. Chatterton's departure from his native city Browning saw as an attempt to break the snares of falsehood which Bristol had woven. In the fact that Chatterton after leaving Bristol resorted to Row-

[55] Sir Walter Scott's anonymous review of the Southey and Cottle edition of Chatterton's works in *The Edinburgh Review*, IV (1804), 217–218, 226.

ley on but one occasion, Browning saw proof that he was winning his way back to Truth:

> *Now would have been indeed the white minute for discov-*
> *eries and forgeries. He was often pressed for matter; had to*
> *solicit all his Bristol acquaintance for contributions (some of*
> *such go under his own name now, possibly); but with the one*
> *exception we have alluded to (affecting for a passage in which*
> *his own destitute condition is too expressly described to admit*
> *of mistake) — the Ballad of Charity —* Rowley was done
> with. (860–867)

Browning has here suited the facts to his case with great ingenuity, but at best his argument is adroit special-pleading that
fits only a part of the evidence. On May 14, in a letter from
which Browning quotes in the Essay, Chatterton wrote his
mother that "had Rowley been a Londoner," he "could have
lived by copying his works." [56] Probably Chatterton forsook
Rowley not because he was struggling toward the ways of
Truth, but because London editors showed no great inclination to publish Bristol antiquities.

Having traced Chatterton's first false step taken in youthful innocence, his gradual entanglement in the meshes of
falsehood, his efforts to return to Truth, and his eventual
abnegation of Rowley through leaving Bristol for London,
Browning evolved an effective conclusion for his prose tragedy. It is in Chatterton's death scene that Browning reveals
himself most clearly as a writer of plays. Like Alfred de
Vigny, Browning felt a need to heighten the drama of Chatterton's last moments by giving his hero a choice between
bread with ignomimy and death with honor. Vigny had solved

[56] *Works*, ed. Willcox, p. 717; Dix, *Life*, p. 270.

the problem by allowing William Beckford, Lord Mayor of London, to offer the poet a place as valet in his household. In actuality, Beckford had never offered anything so promising, and he had preceded Chatterton in death by two months. Browning met the problem with a still bolder leap in both fact and time. The hero of the Essay, though done with Rowley, is tempted to exploit his powers in a final deception; but his moral self rebels. He chooses death rather than further falsehood:

[*Chatterton*], "*knowing that a great genius can effect any thing, endeavoured in the foregoing poems to represent an Enthusiastic Methodist, and intended to send it to Romaine, and impose it on the infatuated world as a reality;*" — *but Now, no sooner is the intellectual effort made than the moral one succeeds, and destroying these poems he determined to kill himself. Every way unsuccessful, every way discouraged, the last scene had come. When he killed himself, his room was found "strewn thick over with torn papers.*" (767–775)

Even in *The Ring and the Book* it would be hard to match this epitome of the strange fusion of history and creative fancy which could take place when Browning made it his business "to explain *fact*." The first half of the passage is a quotation adapted from the note which Chatterton prefixed to his *Will*. Earlier in the Essay (700–736) Browning had already discussed this document. There he had treated it correctly as being written four months prior to the suicide, before Chatterton left Bristol for London. In order to read these words into Chatterton's death scene, Browning not only had to change the time and place in which they were written; he had to divorce them entirely from the context in which they appear. The note in its entirety follows:

N.B. — In a dispute concerning the character of David, Mr. —— argued that he must be a holy man, from the strains of piety that breathe through his whole works — I being of a contrary opinion, and knowing that a great genius can effect any thing, endeavouring in the foregoing Poems *to represent an enthusiastic Methodist, intended to send it to Romaine, and impose it upon the infatuated world as a reality; but thanks to Burgum's generosity, I am now employed in matters of more importance.*

Saturday, April 20, 1770.[57]

Browning's statement that Chatterton destroyed "these poems" in his last moments is, of course, also a product of his creative imagination. There is no evidence that Mrs. Angel or any of her tenants collected and identified the scraps of paper which littered the death chamber. Possibly they were not of great importance. According to his roommate at the Walmsleys', where he had first taken residence in London, Chatterton was in the habit of leaving the floor "covered with pieces of paper not so big as sixpences, into which he had torn what he had been writing before he came to bed." [58]

5

Was Browning in the death scene and elsewhere in the Essay deliberately manipulating the facts to suit his own inter-

[57] Dix, *Life*, p. 235. Willcox (*Works*, p. 622) reads identically save that a period appears after *works*, and *anything* is written solid. Wilson (*Life*, p. 245) pointed out that Chatterton actually wrote *affect every thing*, not *effect any thing*, but the error appears in all printings of the *Will* before 1869.

[58] Croft, *Love and Madness*, p. 193.

pretation? Was he, from one point of view at least, consciously deviating from the "ways of Truth" even in showing that Chatterton at his death was entering upon them? Such a conclusion seems unwarranted. Browning set an almost Quixotic value on personal honesty. He wrote the Essay to draw a more faithful likeness of Chatterton than biographers had achieved; his words make it clear that he believed he had succeeded in doing so.

The following appears a more likely explanation: Although, as will be seen in the notes to this edition, Browning read the detailed accounts of Chatterton's life intensively, he read them with a general plan for Chatterton's conduct already in mind. He was looking for corroborations of his original idea, and his resourceful brain inevitably succeeded in making them out. There is a revealing passage in the Essay which partially explains his method of reading his materials:

It is needless for us here to interpose that our whole argument goes, not upon what Chatterton said, but what he did: it is part of our proof to show that all his distress arose out of the impossibility of his saying any thing to the real purpose. (720–724)

By thus allowing himself on principle to go against the evidence of Chatterton's statements, Browning gave a formidable license to his own powers of insight. Chatterton could in vain, for example, jeer at religious doctrine and proclaim himself no Christian. To Browning, who had determined that such a genius could not but be the "noblest-hearted of mortals," these disclaimers represented only a ruse adopted by Chatterton to conceal his identity with the "Godlie preeste Rowlie." (336–340, 810–835)

47

But Browning did not, of course, actually confine himself to what Chatterton did. Much of his argument is based upon a special reading of what Chatterton wrote and said. Browning was confident of what he would find; a great deal that would not fit his plan for Chatterton's conduct escaped him. Satisfied that his hero went to London solely to free himself from Rowley, Browning sought for, or drew from memory,[59] evidence that Chatterton was fond of his native city and did not leave it for other reasons: "Had he any dislike to Bristol or its inhabitants generally? 'His company pleased universally,' he says: 'he believed he had promised to write to some hundreds of his acquaintance.'" (683–686) In the letter from which he quotes, Browning could have read these sentences:

But to return once more to a place I am sickened to write of, Bristol. Though, as an apprentice, none had greater liberties, yet the thoughts of servitude killed me: now I have that for my labour I always reckoned the first of my pleasures, and have still my liberty. . . I promised, before my departure, to write to some hundreds, I believe; but, what with writing for publications, and going to places of public diversion, which is as absolutely necessary to me as food, I find but little time to write to you. As to Mr. Barrett, Mr. Catcott, Mr. Burgum, &c. &c. they rate literary lumber so low, that I believe an author, in their estimation, must be poor indeed! But here, matters are otherwise; had Rowley been a Londoner, instead of a Bristowyan, I could have lived by copying

[59] Many, though hardly all, of Browning's strangely eclectic quotations from his materials can be explained on the assumption that he quoted from memory and thus divorced sentences or half-sentences from their damaging context. See note 81 to the text of the Essay.

48

his works. — In my humble opinion, I am under very few obligations to any person in Bristol: one, indeed, has obliged me; but as most do, in a manner which makes his obligation no obligation. — My youthful acquaintances will not take it in dudgeon, that I do not write oftener to them, than I believe I shall: but, as I had the happy art of pleasing in conversation, my company was often liked, where I did not like: and to continue a correspondence under such circumstances, would be ridiculous.[60]

Sure of his insight into the true state of Chatterton's feelings, Browning may have found here only an evidence that Chatterton was whistling to keep up his spirits.

At the end of the Essay Browning again describes his method of handling his materials. He implies that he has worked by "balancing conflicting statements, interpreting doubtful passages, and reconciling discrepant utterances." [61] The words have a curious echo in Browning's remark to William Michael Rossetti many years later concerning *The Ring and the Book*. The Old Yellow Book, he said, had offered him a "mass of almost equally balanced evidence," pondering which he arrived at his conception of the characters.[62]

But Browning weighed the conflicting statements of the Old Yellow Book with his own memories and his familiar patterns of thought counting heavily on one side of the scales. Long before he read the truth of Caponsacchi's conduct, an

---

[60] *Works*, ed. Willcox, pp. 715–717.

[61] (900–902) Browning states that in doing so he is following Richard Henry Wilde's method in studying Tasso's character. Actually Wilde could have given him little guidance. See below, pp. 80ff.

[62] *Rossetti Papers, 1862 to 1870* (London, 1903), p. 401.

ideal pattern of chivalric rescue of innocence in distress had, as Dean DeVane has pointed out, deeply engraved itself upon his mind:

> *In his youth he kept ever before him on his desk the picture of Caravaggio's* Andromeda, *"the perfect picture," and in* Pauline *he set that up as the symbol of his faith* (ll. 656–65). *He rested in the faith that "some god . . . would come in thunder from the stars" to save truth in the nick of time from the forces which beset her. He gave this idea expression in his poetry many times.*[63]

In *Count Gismond* and *Colombe's Birthday* in particular, the pattern is a guiding and shaping force. In his own life, "he performed the part of Perseus to Miss Barrett's Andromeda."[64] Pompilia became not only Andromeda but Elizabeth Barrett Browning.[65] To an objective eye, the story of the Old Yellow Book may seem to contain no inspiring truth; Carlyle found it "plain enough . . . the girl and the handsome young priest were lovers."[66] For Browning, the facts fell into a design preconceived and waiting.

In the Essay, as in *The Ring and the Book*, Browning read the facts according to formulas that were already a part of his thinking. He had planned and portrayed the career and

---

[63] *Handbook*, p. 305. DeVane points out that the Pope, also, is a Perseus who "saves truth just in time by his condemnation of the sophistries of evil."

[64] *Ibid.*

[65] See Mrs. Sutherland Orr, *Life and Letters of Robert Browning*, revised by Frederic G. Kenyon (Boston, 1908), pp. 251, 270–272; C. H. Herford, *Robert Browning* (New York, 1905), pp. 169–170, 179; J. E. Shaw, "The 'Donna Angelicata' in *The Ring and the Book*," *Publications of the Modern Language Association*, XLI (1926), 55–81.

[66] *William Allingham, A Diary*, edited by H. Allingham and D. Radford (London, 1907), p. 207.

untimely death of a poet in *Sordello*, published two years before the Essay. His strangely unhistorical reading of Chatterton's "last scene" takes on new and intimate significance in the light of Sordello's story. Like Chatterton, Sordello had been divided against himself, with the intellectual and moral parts of his nature in conflict. Like Chatterton, Sordello had suffered a final temptation and had downed it with a moral effort at the doors of death. The poems which had symbolized Chatterton's temptation lay strewn in fragments about the floor of his death chamber. Sordello died with the badge which would have given him power at the expense of honor trampled beneath his foot. Sordello perished by the stress of his own conflicting emotions. One wonders whether Browning's Chatterton could not have managed without the poison.

But the full and remarkable extent to which Browning remade Chatterton according to patterns that his hand had already practiced must be seen in another work. Though not published until January, 1843, *The Return of the Druses* was completed and offered to Macready, the actor-manager, by the midsummer of 1840.[67] In this play, Browning had portrayed in detail the career of a noble soul who comes to a tragic and untimely death through struggling to free himself from the effects of an early imposture. The correspondences between the hero of Browning's play and the hero of his essay are at times so striking that there is a temptation to harbor suspicions which are not apt to be either scouted or substantiated. Did Browning think of letting Chatterton reveal his truth upon the stage? In any event, Djabal, like Chatterton, (1) takes his first false step in youth, (2) resorts to imposture

[67] DeVane, *Handbook*, pp. 119–120.

because the world will otherwise refuse him the exercise of his talents, (3) succeeds in his deception only because of his intellectual superiority to his credulous audience, (4) finds that his followers prize the accidental rather than the real merit of his work, (5) suffers because he cannot claim as his own his achievements in a borrowed guise, (6) struggles manfully to free himself from the effects of his first false step, (7) makes a partial return to the ways of Truth, but (8) achieves a final victory over falsehood, the moral impulses of his nature triumphing over the intellectual, only in his last moments. These and other similarities between the Essay and *The Return of the Druses* are followed at length in the next chapter.

6

In shaping the Essay, then, Browning rehearsed in its essentials the process by which a quarter of a century later he turned the crude ore of the Old Yellow Book into his most famous poem. Working with a mass of historical data, Browning clearly intended in the Essay, as in *The Ring and the Book*, to "explain *fact*," to champion truth which lay helpless and mangled through the cynicism and obtuseness of professional motive-mongers. Just as clearly he worked in both instances as a romantic poet rather than as an historian. He idealized Chatterton, as he did the Pompilia and the Caponsacchi who were to follow, far above nature; their springs of conduct are to be traced not in Browning's sources but in the patterns already intimately established in his own habits of thought. Yet in the Essay, as in *The Ring and the Book*, he managed so effectively to fuse factual detail with ideal conception that his handiwork has the air and the substance of reality. Such was the peculiar cast of Browning's creative thinking that he could twist fact itself to his artistic ends with a confident hand, assured that even in doing so he was serving the cause of historical truth. By a curious process of self-hypnosis, as traceable in the essay of 1842 as in the great poem of 1868, he was able to wed romanticism and realism, evangelism and naturalism — to weave parables of high spiritual import from the sordid, tangled minutiae of a Holborn suicide or a Roman murder case.

III

FACT AND FORMULA —
THREE STUDIES IN IMPOSTURE

IN the last chapter we saw at some length the relation of
Browning's hero to Chatterton as drawn by his biographers. In this chapter the theme itself is the relation
of the hero of the Essay to two specific characters among
Browning's acknowledged dramatis personae. For Browning
made not one but three ambitious studies of impostors. As
the pivotal member of a clearly defined triad — *The Return
of the Druses*, the Essay on Chatterton, and *Mr. Sludge,
"The Medium"* — the strange account of Chatterton's career
opens a new perspective upon a peculiarly interesting aspect
of Browning's work, his manner of studying tortuous minds
and unraveling complex mental processes. Fitting the Essay
into the course of Browning's work, we are able to trace for
the first time the full extent to which he read and shaped
character in the world about him by patterns already established in his creative thought.

On casual acquaintance, Browning's three heroes — a fifteenth-century Oriental mystic, an eighteenth-century Bristol
poet, a contemporary American spiritualistic medium — can
seem as separate and distinct in personality as in time and
setting. Browning was a resourceful artist with a remarkable
gift for making ideas proceed plausibly and with an effect of
immediacy in the words and actions of his individual charac-

ters. It is only when Djabal, Chatterton, and Sludge are studied in conjunction, and studied with a view to their inner experience rather than to their gestures before the footlights, that they are seen to be brothers under the skin, creations upon the same general design shaped at three successive stages of the author's development.

In *The Return of the Druses*, completed at least by the midsummer of 1840,[1] Browning worked out his prototype for the genus *impostor* unhindered by historical considerations. The hero of this drama is purely the product of his own imagination. G. K. Chesterton, with a fellow artist's discernment, sensed the significance of Djabal for Browning:

> [*Djabal*] *is supremely important in the history of Browning's mind, for he is the first of that great series of the apologiae of apparently evil men, on which the poet was to pour out so much of his imaginative wealth — Djabal, Fra Lippo, Bishop Blougram, Sludge, Prince Hohenstiel-Schwangau, and the hero of* Fifine at the Fair.[2]

Unaware of the existence of Browning's second study of imposture, Chesterton nevertheless caught something of the relation of Djabal to Sludge: ". . . even realising the humanity of a noble impostor like Djabal did not content his erratic hunger for goodness. He went further again, and realised the humanity of a mean impostor like Sludge."[3]

Between these two, as Chesterton could not know, lies the Chatterton of the Essay. But two years later than Browning's first study in point of time, his second shows a striking advance in theory and practice. In theory, indeed, Browning already

[1] DeVane, *A Browning Handbook*, p. 120.
[2] *Robert Browning* (English Men of Letters Series; London, 1906), p. 51.
[3] *Ibid.*, p. 52.

approached maturity. In the essay of 1842 he proposed to effect the anatomy of an actual rather than a hypothetical mind; he attempted to thread the ways of a complex mentality to show that a thirst for good had motivated his subject's most devious actions. This is the essential theory of his studies of supposedly shifty characters from the Essay onward. The difference between his diagnosis of Chatterton's truth and his diagnosis of Sludge's truth in 1864 is a question of degree rather than kind. There was considerably less virtue in Sludge, presented at his best, and apology became tantamount to exposure.

In practice as opposed to theory, Browning in the Essay passed from creating character by use of imaginary scenes and incidents to creating character with almost equal arbitrariness by use of factual detail. Employing the reading of imposture which he had formulated for the *Druses*, Browning proceeded to make it manifest itself in the particulars of Chatterton biography. In his second canvas for his special gallery, Browning followed the general lineaments of his first portrait while he ostensibly painted from life.

When, two decades later, Browning made his third study of imposture, he worked by the same general process as in the Essay. There is a more vivid impression of reality in the mature canvas, a stronger sense of immediacy through the impact of effective detail. But the portrait of David Sludge clearly was painted by the strangely reminiscent artist who had done Thomas Chatterton. In the Essay, Horace Walpole's statement that "all of the house of forgery are relations" is held up for condemnation; but Browning's three studies in imposture, taken together, demonstrate a theorem very like it.

I

The setting of *The Return of the Druses* is a Mediterranean island on which the Syrian tribe lives in subjection to the Knights of Rhodes. The time is the fifteenth century. Browning's hero is a youthful Druse who incites his people to revolt against their overlords so that he can lead them back to the home of their fathers beneath the Cedars of Lebanon. The incidents of the play naturally differ considerably from the incidents of the Essay. A love plot complicates the *Druses*, and Djabal is at the outset half-persuaded of the truth of his own imposture. But these are special conditions of the specific plot. It is the unfolding of Djabal's mind in the course of the drama that chiefly concerns us as it obviously did Browning.

Waiving accidents of time and setting, Djabal's essential tragedy is the tragedy of a lofty mind whose exceptional powers by their very bent and nature render it susceptible to a special malady — a fatal maladjustment of the intellectual and the moral faculties. Unable to exercise his great intellectual powers by direct and open means, Djabal resorts to imposture. His moral impulses, however, are as strong as his intellectual. While his intellectual self drives him powerfully to carry out the plan which it has conceived, a plan already prospering and promising success, his moral self drives him as powerfully to renounce falsehood and destroy all that he has built. This is Djabal's story, and it is also Chatterton's as Browning portrays it in his imaginative and unhistorical Essay.

Chatterton's death, it will be remembered, immediately followed on a final struggle between the two parts of his nature.

Tearing up the poems which his intellectual self had intended to foist upon the world as the work of an Enthusiastic Methodist, he decided to kill himself. Since the *Druses* is a drama, Djabal is able, before using his dagger, to diagnose the malady which drives him to self-slaughter. His "Arab heart" has at all times during his career of imposture frustrated his "Frank brain" schooled in the ways of deception during his years of exile among the French, and the conflict can be resolved only in suicide:

> *I with my Arab instinct, thwarted ever*
> *By my Frank policy, — and with, in turn,*
> *My Frank brain, thwarted by my Arab heart —*
> *While these remained in equipoise, I lived*
> *— Nothing; had either been predominant,*
> *As a Frank schemer or an Arab mystic,*
> *I had been something; — now, each has destroyed*
> *The other.* (V, 270–277)

At their beginning as in their ending, the two courses of imposture run parallel paths. Djabal's words (II, 169) could fit without change into the Essay. In both careers "child's-carelessness" came to "prove manhood's crime." It was Chatterton's misfortune as it was Djabal's

> *To have wandered through the world,*
> *Sown falsehood, and thence reaped now scorn,*
> *now faith.* (II, 2–3)

Browning's defense of Chatterton's comparative innocence in beginning the Rowley forgeries rests upon three points. First, Chatterton could not obtain a hearing for his poetry and recognition for his true merit by any means other than imposture.

(341–377) Second, Chatterton's devices were not those of a hardened falsifier of truth: "There was, after all, no such elaborate deception about any of them." (380–381) Third, Chatterton would have been detected and set upon the right path once more had his fellow Bristolians not been amazingly credulous: "Indeed, had there only happened to be a single individual of ordinary intelligence among his intimates, the event must assuredly have fallen out differently." (381–384)

These are the very points which Browning had already allowed Djabal to urge for the relative innocence of his beginnings in imposture. Because he could not otherwise persuade the Druses to acknowledge his leadership, he had found it necessary to proclaim himself Hakeem, their god incarnate, who, according to prophecy, would appear to lead them back to their ancestral home:

> *I said, "Without*
> *"A miracle this cannot be" — I said*
> *"Be there a miracle!"* (IV, 65–67)

But he had attempted no elaborate deception. A few tricks of magic learned in exile enabled him to master his credulous tribesmen:

> *A few secrets*
> *That would not easily affect the meanest*
> *Of the crowd there, could wholly subjugate*
> *The best of our poor tribe.* (IV, 81–84)

Chatterton was betrayed by the success of his deception, which put increasing barriers in the way of confession. He found a "worse than St. Anna dungeon" was "every hour . . . building up more surely between him and the common earth and skies." (219–221) "Day followed day, and found him only more and more deeply involved." (468–470) Browning had already plotted Djabal's course along the same lines. The hero of the *Druses* could with great justice exclaim, "All things conspire to hound me on." (III, 158)

· Bristol valued only antiquity in Chatterton's forgeries, and saw little merit in them as poetry. (361–366) Chatterton realized that if he discarded the guise of antiquity he would lose his audience: "Give that up, and all was given . . . " (367) He had lost his own personality in Rowley, and the wide gap between what he did and what he could demand recognition for doing was a major affliction: "For there was the sense of his being the author of the transcendent chorus to Freedom, or the delicious roundelay in *Ella*; ever at fierce variance with the pitiful claim he was entitled to make in the character of their mere transcriber." (450–453) Browning must have had no great difficulty in coming to this analysis of Chatterton's state of mind. He had made the same diagnosis, with names changed, for the *Druses*. What Rowley was to Chatterton, Hakeem was to Djabal. As the Bristolians saw the antiquity of Rowley rather than the poetry of Chatterton and held the true author between the alternatives of giving all up or remaining in the character of transcriber, so the Druses valued the miracles of Hakeem rather than Djabal's leadership and forced him to choose between losing his following and remaining the mere body through which Hakeem spoke. Like Chatterton, Djabal chafed beneath his mask:

> *Hakeem? Why the God?*
> *Shout, rather, "Djabal, Youssof's child, thought slain*
> *"With his whole race, the Druses' Sheikhs, this Prefect*
> *"Endeavoured to extirpate — saved, a child,*

"Returns from traversing the world, a man,
"Able to take revenge, lead back the march
"To Lebanon" — so shout, and who gainsays?
But now, because delusion mixed itself
Insensibly with this career, all's changed!
Have I brought Venice to afford us convoy?
"True — but my jugglings wrought that!" Put I heart
Into our people where no heart lurked? — "Ah,
"What cannot an impostor do!"   (II, 17–29)

Even after he had made progress in his struggles toward truth, Chatterton found his abilities at imposture a strong temptation: "Now no one can suppose, and we are far from asserting, that at word of command, Chatterton wholly put aside the old habit of imposing upon people — if that is to be the phrase." (751–754) But Browning was unwilling to allow the phrase. He preferred to think Chatterton's motive was no petty desire to defraud, but a lofty though misguided ambition to rule less robust natures than his own through application of an old and established principle:

But this "imposing upon people" has not always that basest meaning. It is old as the world itself, the tendency of certain spirits to subdue each man by perceiving what will master him, by straightway supplying it from their own resources, and so obtaining, as tokens of success, his admiration, or fear, or wonder. It has been said even that classes of men are immediately ruled in no other way. (754–761)

Djabal also had felt the temptation to go on turning his powers to account. Even after he has shared his secret with Anael, his betrothed, he thinks, momentarily, of continuing his falsehood as a means of governing the Druses beneficently once they have regained their homeland. He defends the action by citing the general principle which Browning two years later was to allow to Chatterton:

> *What if we reign together? — if we keep*
> *Our secret for the Druses' good? — by means*
> *Of even their superstition, plant in them*
> *New life? I learn from Europe: all who seek*
> *Man's good must awe men, by such means as these.*[4]
>
> (IV, 122–126)

In their habitual moods, however, both Chatterton and Djabal condone their present actions to themselves by promising that once the immediate end is gained they will put aside falsehood forever. This idea is strong in the minds of all three of Browning's impostors. Sludge, as we shall see, offers it as the key to his whole career. Browning was convinced that Chatterton would have dropped Rowley and led an honest life if he had succeeded with Walpole: "Of nothing are we so thoroughly persuaded as that these attempts were the predetermined last acts of a course of dissimulation he would fain discard for ever — on their success." (505–508) Browning stresses this point in his interpretation of Chatterton, developing his relation to Walpole at length and in detail. (508–640) Here as elsewhere, however, Browning read the facts to a pattern that he had already practised. Djabal's

---

[4] As Dean DeVane has already shown (*Browning's Parleyings: The Autobiography of a Mind*, Yale University Press, 1927, pp. 148ff.), Djabal's theory of statesmanship appears as well in *Colombe's Birthday*; *Bishop Blougram's Apology*; *Mr. Sludge, "The Medium"*; *Prince Hohenstiel-Schwangau*; and the *Parleying with George Bubb Dodington*. Sludge's application of the idea will be discussed in detail below.

thoughts, like Chatterton's, had been colored throughout his course by the idea of reform once his imposture had succeeded. His cry when his moral self objected was "not now, my soul, draw back, at least! Not now!" (III, 159) Except for momentary temptation, he was resolved to abandon Hakeem as soon as the Druses were safe beneath the Cedars of Lebanon:

> *The course is plain, howe'er obscure all else.*
> *Once offer this tremendous sacrifice,*
> *Prevent what else will be irreparable,*
> *Secure these transcendental helps, regain*
> *The Cedars — then let all dark clear itself!*
>
> (III, 160–165)

Djabal's career is complicated by his love for Anael. He thinks of extricating himself from the meshes of falsehood by quitting the island, but his love is too great to allow him to express his thought in anything stronger than the subjunctive. (II, 300) Chatterton, unencumbered by an Anael, was able to leave Bristol, thus "disengaging himself from the still increasing trammels of his daily life of enforced deceit." (489–490) Even in London, however, the way back to truth was not easy. In both the Essay and *The Return of the Druses*, the hero's closing actions are a courageous and ultimately successful effort to renounce falsehood in spite of increasing temptations to reap the rewards of imposture. Chatterton forsook Rowley at the time when Rowley could have offered him most:

> *The point is,* No more Rowley. *His connexion with the Magazines had commenced with Rowley — they had readily inserted portions of his poems — and we cannot conceive a*

more favourable field of enterprise than London would have afforded, had he been disposed to go on with the fabrication. No prying intimates, nor familiar townsmen, in Mrs. Angel's quiet lodging! He had the ear, too, of many booksellers. Now would have been indeed the white minute [5] *for discoveries and forgeries.* (853–861)

In the face of growing incentives for continuing Hakeem, Djabal makes his confession to Anael, vowing that

> *The Past*
> *Is past: my false life shall henceforth show true.*
> (IV, 118–119)

But like Chatterton he wins his final victory over falsehood only in death. He clearly states the lesson of his life:

> *With truth and purity go other gifts,*
> *All gifts come clustering to that.* (V, 361–362)

To appreciate the full extent to which Browning made over Chatterton in the image of Djabal, one must remember that the Chatterton of the biographers was a youth of strangely mixed disposition who showed not his worst but his best side in the creation of the Rowley poems, who wrote scurrilous and often hardly printable satires, who boasted of his real or

---

[5] The "white minute" for Chatterton's decision adds another to the long list of critical minutes in Browning's works. Compare *The Return of the Druses* (II, 31–36):

> Falsehood! Thou shalt not keep thy hold on me!
> — Nor even get a hold on me! 'T is now —
> This day — hour — minute — 't is as here I stand
> On the accursed threshold of the Prefect,
> That I am found deceiving and deceived!
> And now what do I?

imagined amorous conquests, and who, far from regretting his impostures, railed in his verses at the men who had made themselves his dupes. Browning could have absorbed scarcely a trace of his interpretation as viewed in this section from the biographies which he consulted. The fatal conflict between the intellectual and moral parts of his hero's nature, the high aims which guided his first false step, the unhappiness resulting from his inability to claim his own work, the resolve to reform once he had succeeded with Walpole, the moral motives which led him to leave Bristol, the final temptation immediately preceding the suicide, the ultimate triumph of his moral over his intellectual self are to be found only in Browning's portrait. Taken together, they depict a character very different from the Chatterton that Bristol and London knew. Even in Browning's handling, Chatterton falls short of the lofty altruism of Djabal, who compromised with falsehood to save his people, and returned to truth under the influence of a selfless love. But in nearly every particular where Browning departs from biography his hand seems clearly to be guided by memories of the character that he had evolved and portrayed in the *Druses* two years earlier.

2

Mr. Sludge, "*The Medium*," was published in *Dramatis Personae* (1864) and written probably in 1859 or 1860.[6] In 1855 Browning had been present at a séance conducted by D. D. Home (or Hume), the American spiritualistic medium. Browning was openly suspicious of the proceedings. After he was refused admittance to a second séance, he publicly de-

[6] DeVane, *Handbook*, p. 271.

nounced Home on more than one occasion as a charlatan. Home's continued practice in England and on the continent added oil to the fire.[7] *Mr. Sludge, "The Medium,"* is Browning's vent for his intense antipathy toward Sludge's original. But the poem is not merely satire. It is an attempt to trace Sludge's own point of view regarding his tortuous career, as Sludge himself bears witness near the end of his monologue:

> *I know I acted wrongly: still, I've tried*
> *What I could say in my excuse, — to show*
> *The devil's not all devil.* (1481–1483)

Though he has obviously developed into a case-hardened villain by the time that he confides his career to Hiram H. Horsefall, Sludge the self-apologist makes a strong plea for the comparative innocence of his early beginnings as an impostor and the gradualness of his descent along the primrose path.

Like Djabal, and like Browning's Chatterton, Sludge suffered the malady which attends impostors. His moral self had at no time been so robust as to set him struggling in earnest toward the ways of truth; nevertheless it had a real existence, and it had waged a persistent though losing war with the intellectual part of him:

> *There's something in real truth (explain who can!)*
> *One casts a wistful eye at, like the horse*
> *Who mopes beneath stuffed hay-racks and won't munch*
> *Because he spies a corn-bag: hang that truth,*

---

[7] For a fuller account of Browning's experiences with Home than is given here, see DeVane, *Handbook*, pp. 272–276, and W. L. Phelps, "Robert Browning on Spiritualism," *Yale Review*, XXIII (1933), 125–138.

It spoils all dainties proffered in its place!
I've felt at times when, cockered, cosseted
And coddled by the aforesaid company . . .
I've felt a child; only, a fractious child
That, dandled soft by nurse, aunt, grandmother,
Who keep him from the kennel, sun and wind,
Good fun and wholesome mud, — enjoined be sweet,
And comely and superior, — eyes askance
The ragged sons o' the gutter at their game,
Fain would be down with them i' the thick o' the filth,
Making dirt-pies, laughing free, speaking plain,
And calling granny the grey old cat she is.
I've felt a spite, I say, at you, at them,
Huggings and humbug — gnashed my teeth to mark
A decent dog pass! It's too bad, I say,
Ruining a soul so!   (382–403)

The maladjustment of the two parts of his nature is the essential story of Sludge even as it is the story of Djabal and of
Chatterton. The tragic ending is merely of another sort —
a moral suicide. It is in his account of his early years that
Sludge is closest to Djabal and closer still to Chatterton.

Sludge is in his way, indeed, something of a poet. The
ware which he offered his early patrons was curiously similar
to Chatterton's. The Bristol poet had resorted to "muniment-room treasures and yellow-roll discoveries" in a comparatively innocent attempt to enhance the value of his work,
an attempt that "by no means exceeded in relative hardihood
the mildest possible annexing — whatever the modern author's name may be — to the current poetry or prose of the
time." (207–209) Sludge had offered a bright though spe-

cious gold which he was peculiarly capable of coining — fiction plated with a pretense to truth:

> *Strictly, it's what good people style untruth;*
> *But yet, so far, not quite the full-grown thing:*
> *It's fancying, fable-making, nonsense-work —*
> *What never meant to be so very bad —*
> *The knack of story-telling, brightening up*
> *Each dull old bit of fact that drops its shine.*
>
> (188–193)

He defends even his mature practice as a sort of poetical fable-making, a bringing to life of happier realms not unlike Chatterton's bringing to life of Rowley's world:

> *Why, here's the Golden Age, old Paradise*
> *Or new Eutopia! Here's true life indeed,*
> *And the world well won now, mine for the first time!*
>
> *And all this might be, may be, and with good help*
> *Of a little lying shall be: so, Sludge lies!*
> *Why, he's at worst your poet who sings how Greeks*
> *That never were, in Troy that never was,*
> *Did this or the other impossible great thing!*
> *He's Lowell — it's a world (you smile applause),*
> *Of his own invention — wondrous Longfellow,*
> *Surprising Hawthorne! Sludge does more than they,*
> *And acts the books they write: the more his praise!*
>
> (1431–1442)

At the start of his career Sludge had to face the problem of fable-makers in general; he required hearers and patrons. His resourcefulness in overcoming this difficulty and his comments upon his method of solving it suggest that he may have taken lessons from the Essay on Chatterton. There he could have learned that the world is usually hostile to the offerings of beginners in the field. He could have learned, too, that beginners typically attempt to circumvent the prejudices of the world against them by resorting to a pretense of one kind or another:

And so instinctively does the Young Poet feel that his desire for this kind of self-enfranchisement will be resisted as a matter of course, that we will venture to say, in nine cases out of ten his first assumption of the licence will be made in a borrowed name. . . So is the way gracefully facilitated for Reader and Hearer finding themselves in a new position with respect to each other. (350–360)

Chatterton had facilitated the way to his hearers through the myth of Rowley. In choosing the borrowed guise of an earlier age, he happened to touch the particular weakness of Bristol Literati, an uncritical and faddish antiquarianism. Chatterton's account of the Mayor's "first passing over the Old Bridge, taken from an old manuscript" caught their fancy at once:

The attention of — what are called in the accounts we have seen — "the literati of Bristol," was excited. Application was made to the publisher for a sight of the surprising and interesting original. No such thing was forthcoming; but the curiosity of Literati must be appeased. (240–244)

Having traced the original to Chatterton and tried threats to no avail, the Literati managed through milder usage and promises to elicit from Chatterton a confession that the manuscript from which he had quoted was one of many which his father had taken from a coffer in the Church of St. Mary, Redcliff. (244–256)

Sludge likewise perceived the need of facilitating the way to hearers, and revealed his powers at fable-making under the protection of a borrowed guise. Less innocently than Chatterton he chose a garb designed to touch the particular weakness of his audience. Had he tried them in any other quarter, he would, he knew, have experienced what Browning in the Essay terms the "popular jealousy of allowing this privilege [of imaginative expression] to the first claimant." (349–350) Sludge describes this aspect of popular psychology in homelier language:

> . . . *well, suppose*
> *A poor lad, say a help's son in your house,*
> *Listening at keyholes, hears the company*
> *Talk grand of dollars, V-notes, and so forth,*
> *How hard they are to get, how good to hold,*
> *How much they buy, — if, suddenly, in pops he —*
> *"I've got a V-note!" — what do you say to him?*
> *What's your first word which follows your last kick?*
> *"Where did you steal it, rascal?" That's because*
> *He finds you, fain would fool you, off your perch,*
> *Not on the special piece of nonsense, sir,*
> *Elected your parade-ground . . .* (97–108)

But on their special perch — in this instance, spiritualism — all was different:

> *But let the same lad hear you talk as grand*
> *At the same keyhole, you and company,*

Of signs and wonders, the invisible world;
How wisdom scouts our vulgar unbelief
More than our vulgarest credulity;
How good men have desired to see a ghost,
What Johnson used to say, what Wesley did,
Mother Goose thought, and fiddle-diddle-dee: —
If he break in with, "Sir, I saw a ghost!"
Ah, the ways change!   (130–139)

As the Literati drew out Chatterton, so the amateurs of the occult draw out Sludge:

           He finds you perched and prim;
It's a conceit of yours that ghosts may be:
There's no talk now of cow-hide. "Tell it out!
"Don't fear us! Take your time and recollect!
"Sit down first: try a glass of wine, my boy!
"And, David, (is not that your Christian name?)
"Of all things, should this happen twice — it may —
"Be sure, while fresh in mind, you let us know!"
                        (139–146)

Like Chatterton's Literati, they indulge their own credulity to the utmost. Chatterton's first falsehoods had "no such elaborate deception about any of them." (381) "That there should have been a controversy for ten minutes about the genuineness of any ten verses of 'Rowley' is a real disgrace to the scholarship of the age in which such a thing took place." (260–263) Sludge's tale faltered, but his hearers filled the gaps and countenanced all:

Does the boy blunder, blurt out this, blab that,
Break down in the other, as beginners will?

All's candour, all's considerateness — "*No haste!*
"*Pause and collect yourself! We understand!*
"*That's the bad memory, or the natural shock,*
"*Or the unexplained* phenomena!"   (147–152)

Chatterton's patrons "took great interest in the yellow streaks, and verse written like prose without stops; less interest in the poetry; and in Chatterton least, or none at all!" (409–412) Sludge's patrons viewed him as indifferently:

"*What's a 'medium'? He's a means,*
"*Good, bad, indifferent, still the only means*
"*Spirits can speak by; he may misconceive,*
"*Stutter and stammer, — he's their Sludge and drudge.*"
        (332–335)

In the Essay Browning tells us that "at every advance in such a career [as Chatterton's], the impossibility of continuing in the spirit of the outset grows more and more apparent." (212–214) A "few untoward circumstances seem to have effectually determined and given stability to what else had not impossibly proved a mere boy's fancy, destined to go as lightly as it came." (231–234) Once the Literati had seized upon him, Chatterton was pledged to antiquity. "Give that up, and all was given; and poor Chatterton could not give all up. He could only determine for the future to produce Ellas and Godwyns, and other 'beauteous pieces'." (367–369) And so: "Day followed day, and found him only more and more deeply involved." (468–470)

Sludge's story follows the same pattern. He tells us so with the aid of a metaphor from the swimming hole. His first venture in fable-making had entailed no commitment to the

ways of falsehood. While one foot made the experiment, the
other kept him safe on dry land:

> *'T is but a foot in the water and out again;*
> *Not that duck-under which decides your dive.*
> *Note this, for it's important: listen why.* (198–200)

It was his patrons who pushed him off the solid bank for a
total "duck-under" in downright lying:

> *I'll prove, you push on David till he dives*
> *And ends the shivering.* (201–202)

> *And then return to David finally,*
> *Lies seven-feet thick about his first half-inch.*
> *Here's a choice birth o' the supernatural,*
> *Poor David's pledged to! You've employed no tool*
> *That laws exclaim at, save the devil's own,*
> *Yet screwed him into henceforth gulling you*
> *To the top o' your bent, — all out of one half-lie!*
> (241–247)

Even Chatterton, once under way, found that before he could
"extricate himself from the worse than St. Anna dungeon
which every hour was building up more surely between him
and the common earth and skies, so much was to be dared and
done!" (219–222) Sludge, with his less courageous soul,
saw no possible rift in the walls closing about him:

> *You'd prove firmer in his place?*
> *You'd find the courage, — that first flurry over,*
> *That mild bit of romancing-work at end, —*
> *To interpose with "It gets serious, this;*
> *"Must stop here. Sir, I saw no ghost at all.*

"Inform your friends I made . . . well, fools of them,
"And found you ready-made. I've lived in clover
"These three weeks: take it out in kicks of me!"
I doubt it. Ask your conscience!   (250–258)

Yet Sludge's moral self, if we are to take his words seriously, was not wholly vanquished. Like Djabal, who had vowed to reject Hakeem once the Druses were home again, and like Chatterton, who would have given up falsehood for an honest life had he succeeded with Walpole, Sludge kept his conscience narcotized in the present with a promise of future reform:

I've always vowed, after the minute's lie,
And the end's gain, — truth should be mine henceforth.
This goes to the root o' the matter, sir, — this plain
Plump fact: accept it and unlock with it
The wards of many a puzzle!   (1340–1344)

Sludge shifts immediately to other ground, but here also he seems to translate the ideas of Djabal and Chatterton into the argot which suits his nature:

                              Or, finally,
Why should I set so fine a gloss on things?
What need I care? I cheat in self-defence,
And there's my answer to a world of cheats!
Cheat? To be sure, sir! What's the world worth else?
Who takes it as he finds, and thanks his stars?
Don't it want trimming, turning, furbishing up
And polishing over? Your so-styled great men,
Do they accept one truth as truth is found,
Or try their skill at tinkering?   (1344–1353)

Chatterton, Browning tells us, must often in the company of Bristol's Thistlethwaites and Burgums "have felt a certain power he had, lying dormant there, of turning their natures to his own account." (765–767) He had been tempted to follow the age-old "tendency of certain spirits to subdue each man by perceiving what will master him, by straightway supplying it from their own resources, and so obtaining, as tokens of success, his admiration, or fear, or wonder." (756–760)[8] Chatterton triumphed over the temptation. Sludge likewise knew this method of subduing men and gaining mastery over them. Less scrupulous, he throve by applying his knowledge to his special abilities. With all his spirit-world to draw upon, he found what men most desired, and dominated them by supplying it from his own resources:

> *I cheat, and what's the happy consequence?*
> *You find full justice straightway dealt you out,*
> *Each want supplied, each ignorance set at ease,*
> *Each folly fooled. No life-long labour now*
> *As the price of worse than nothing! No mere film*
> *Holding you chained in iron, as it seems,*
> *Against the outstretch of your very arms*
> *And legs i' the sunshine moralists forbid!*
> *What would you have? Just speak and, there,*
>   *you see!*
> *You're supplemented, made a whole at last,*
> *Bacon advises, Shakespeare writes you songs,*
> *And Mary Queen of Scots embraces you.*
>
> (1397–1409)

[8] Djabal also knew this method of dominating men. See above, pp. 61–62.

The differences between Chatterton and Sludge are, of course, as apparent as their similarities. Chatterton, failing with Walpole, left Bristol to spurn falsehood and die in the ways of Truth. Sludge, failing with Horsefall, left Boston in search of another dupe. But Sludge had had a like starting-point in innocence; he had followed a similar path into error, the victim no less than the deceiver of culpably credulous patrons. Even when imposture became his habit, an anemic but persistent yearning after virtue spoiled the rewards of falsehood. In tracing Sludge's early beginnings as an impostor and in following the devious turns by which Sludge later reconciled his practice to his conscience, Browning clearly let his pen follow old patterns.

3

Browning considered himself an accurate historian of the inner life, a psychologist of the human soul. His three studies in imposture, seen in conjunction, show with new clarity how Browning actually construed character in the world about him. The Essay on Chatterton intended a plain view of Chatterton's mental and spiritual experience, something which biographers had been unable to reach. *Mr. Sludge, "The Medium,"* for all its implied satire, intended a plain view of a spiritualistic medium's tortuous thinking. But the formula for a career of imposture which Browning had already planned and used in *The Return of the Druses* was strong upon him when he came to interpret Chatterton's character for the Essay. In turn the Chatterton of the Essay became a model for his revelation of Sludge's inner history.

Browning's title to peculiar and extra-poetic virtues as a

psychologist is still urged. He occasionally has attributed to him a unique "power of psychological dissection," [9] or a work of his is shown to be "a vade mecum of psychiatric and spiritual guidance" for those who suffer from "the spiritual *malaise* of the modern 'civilized' world." [10] The Essay allows us to see more clearly than before that Browning was in manner and method neither a scientist nor an intuitive psychoanalyst. Despite his sincere conviction that he penetrated men's minds and laid bare the secrets of the soul, Browning largely created what he dissected. For all his emphasis upon the minutiae that make up men's daily living, his stress upon the details of human conduct, his elaborate show of analysis of characteristic thought patterns, Browning worked as an artist and produced poetry rather than case histories. He drew nature as he saw it from his subjective point of sight. More than most literary artists, he let old habits of composition guide his hand in new portraits even when he professed to paint from life. Browning was a forerunner of the poetry rather than the science or the religion of psychology. As a master at conceiving subtle intellects and portraying their twists and turnings with fine brushwork and adroit use of effective detail, he is on high and firm ground. Perhaps the most impressive fact of his three studies in imposture is the remarkable versatility and resourcefulness with which he made the formula of the *Druses* come to convincing life in the factual detail of the two studies that followed.

[9] B. G. MacCarthy, *The Psychology of Genius: Studies in Browning* (University of London Press, 1936), p. vii.

[10] Stewart Walker Holmes, "Browning's *Sordello* and Jung: Browning's *Sordello* in the Light of Jung's Theory of Types," *Publications of the Modern Language Association*, LVI (1941), 758.

IV

SPECIAL-PLEADING
IN THE LABORATORY

A FORTNIGHT after the publication of *Prince Hohen-stiel-Schwangau, Saviour of Society* (1871) Browning wrote his friend Isa Blagden:

By this time you have got my little book and seen for your-self whether I make the best or worst of the case. I think in the main, he [Napoleon III] meant to do what I say, and, but for the weakness, grown more apparent in these last years than formerly, would have done what I say he did not.[1]

In his next letter to Miss Blagden, Browning added concern-ing this monologue: ". . . it is just what I imagine the man might, if he pleased, say for himself."[2] Nearly thirty years earlier, in the Essay on Chatterton, Browning had tried his first experiment in making the best of a case and revealing what a character who had been condemned by the world might "say for himself" against the world's interpretation of him.

Browning was happy in his choice of a first client. As we have seen, he believed that Chatterton had a valid defense against the allegations of cynical biographers. Browning ar-gued with earnestness and conviction; he was confident of

[1] *Letters of Robert Browning to Miss Isa Blagden*, arranged by A. J. Armstrong (Baylor University Press, 1923), p. 196.
[2] *Ibid.*, p. 197.

78

winning his case. Later he tackled more difficult subjects. In such notable exercises in special-pleading as *Bishop Blougram's Apology* (1855), *Mr. Sludge, "The Medium"* (1864), the monologues of Guido in *The Ring and the Book* (1868–69), *Prince Hohenstiel-Schwangau* (1871), *Fifine at the Fair* (1872), and *Red Cotton Night-Cap Country* (1873), he pleaded the cases of less admirable characters and argued their briefs without the intention of securing a full acquittal. In all but the last-named poem he employed the dramatic monologue, allowing his characters to defend their courses of action in their own words. Nevertheless Browning's procedure in these later works remained in most respects the procedure which he had used to defend Chatterton in 1842.

Even before the Essay, Browning had been tentatively feeling his way toward a special type of character study. In *The Return of the Druses* he had two years earlier carried his inclination for portraying tortuous mental processes as far as the drama could take him. Farther, indeed, in the opinion of William Charles Macready, who concluded upon reading the play that Browning's intellect was "not quite clear" and that the author of this drama would *"never write again* — to any purpose." [3] The fact was that Browning had fastened upon the general subject matter of his later studies before he had seen the need for a special manner of presenting it. By 1842 he had solved his problem. In the Essay he exhibited what may be called his system of special-pleading — a method of portraying character based upon what a man might "say for himself" against the world's misinterpretation of his conduct.

[3] *The Diaries of William Charles Macready, 1833–1851,* edited by William Toynbee (London, 1912), II, 72.

The Essay, this chapter will attempt to show, was Browning's laboratory experiment in the process of special-pleading. Writing anonymously and writing in prose, he was able to put his ideas into practice with unusual freedom. There is a good deal of evidence that he was fully conscious of trying innovations in presenting his defense of Chatterton. To view the matter clearly, however, it is necessary to lay a ghost of Browning's own making. For Browning in pleading Chatterton's case professed merely to apply the lessons that he had learned from Richard Henry Wilde.

I

It seems certain that Browning first undertook the task of preparing an article for *The Foreign Quarterly Review* with the purpose of writing a review of Wilde's study of Tasso.[4] The title of Wilde's work alone heads the Essay. It is not until the seventh paragraph that Browning mentions the recently published volumes on Chatterton which serve him as a starting point for his discussion of the English poet. His words at this juncture are revealing:

Thinking thus, and grieving over what must be admitted to be the scantiness of the piece of sunshine here, and the narrow and not very novel track it would alone serve to lead us into, — a book was sent to us on a subject not very different from Mr. Wilde's, but on which the service he has sought to render to the memory of Tasso has not hitherto been attempted for a memory more foully outraged. (113–119)

[4] *Conjectures and Researches concerning the Love, Madness, and Imprisonment of Torquato Tasso* (New York, 1842).

One wonders whether the book "was sent" to Browning by John Forster. If so, Forster was at the outset of his editorship deviating from the previous policy of his periodical and from his own later practice, for the scope of the *Foreign Quarterly* did not include reviews of English books upon English authors. Probably the alteration in subject matter was Browning's own idea. Grieved at the scantiness of new material in Wilde's work, and seeing no particularly interesting track for further discussion of Tasso, he had found in Willcox's edition of Chatterton, prefaced by a new biography of the poet, a convenient means of turning into more fertile fields.

But though Browning speaks lightly of Wilde's subject matter,[5] he professes the highest regard for Wilde's method of handling his material. He praises the American writer especially for confining his study to a single aspect of Tasso's life:

> *Such as it is, however, in what Mr. Wilde has done, he has gone the right way to work and done it well. He has steadily restricted himself to the single point in question [whether Tasso loved and was beloved by the Princess of Este]. . . Still it is but a point; and Mr. Wilde has not perhaps done less gracefully and wisely in leaving the rest untouched, than in accomplishing so thoroughly the task he took in hand. He relies upon his subject; is sure of the service he can render by an efficacious treatment of thus much of it; nor entertains any fear lest the bringing in a Before and After, with which he has no immediate concern, should be thought necessary to give interest to the At Present on which he feels he can labour to*

---

[5] "How much that establishes old convictions," Browning exclaims at one point (80–81), "and how little that is even supplementary to them, have we here!"

advantage. We suspect that if we would make any material progress in knowledge of this description, such works must be so undertaken. (82–101)

And Browning proposes to follow Wilde's method in his own attempt to throw a new light upon Chatterton's career:

As the whole of Mr. Wilde's argument may be said to include itself in his commentary upon the opening couplet of the first Sonnet of the collection of Rime,

"True were the loves and transports which I sung,"

so let us say of the Englishman, that his were far from that untruth, that absence of reality, so constantly charged against them. In a word, poor Chatterton's life was not the Lie it is so universally supposed to have been; nor did he "perish in the pride" of refusing to surrender Falsehood and enter on the ways of Truth. We can show, we think, and by some such process as Mr. Wilde adopts in regard to Tasso, that he had already entered on those ways when he was left, without a helping hand, to sink and starve as he might. And to this single point we shall as far as possible restrict ourselves. (136–149)

In the final paragraph of the Essay Browning again acknowledges Wilde as his preceptor:

Thus much has been suggested by Mr. Wilde's method with Tasso. As by balancing conflicting statements, interpreting doubtful passages, and reconciling discrepant utterances, he has examined whether Tasso was true or false, loved or did not love the Princess of Este, was or was not beloved by her,

—so have we sought, from similar evidences, if Chatterton was towards the end of his life hardening himself in deception or striving to cast it off. (899–906)

Browning is so much impressed with the possibilities of this method for revealing the true natures of men whom the world has misunderstood that he ends the Essay with an exhortation:

Let others apply in like manner our inquiry to other great spirits partially obscured, and they will but use us — we hope more effectually — as we have used these able and interesting volumes. (906–909)

Two questions arise from the statements just reviewed and demand to be answered. First, why did Browning give such enthusiastic praise to Wilde's method of working? Second, did Browning actually follow Wilde's method in his own study of Chatterton? The answer to the first question is not far to seek. Even in *Pauline* (1833), his first published poem, Browning had been concerned primarily with analysis of character. In the preface to *Paracelsus* (1835) he had stated his intention of discarding "the operation of persons and events" and "an external machinery of incidents" in order to "display somewhat minutely the mood itself in its rise and progress" within the mind of Paracelsus. In the preface to *Strafford* (1837) Browning proposed to reveal "Action in Character, rather than Character in Action" in his drama. *Sordello* (1840), *The Return of the Druses* (completed by the midsummer of 1840), and *Pippa Passes* (1841) show a continued desire to subordinate external incident in order to lay all possible stress upon the intense study of character. In Wilde's principle of limiting himself to "the single point in question," a single important issue in Tasso's career, and in Wilde's method of analyzing Tasso's nature by "balancing conflicting statements, interpreting doubtful passages, and reconciling discrepant utterances" — by laying all possible stress upon Tasso's inner history as evidenced in his writings rather than upon the external machinery of incident stressed by biographers — Browning could hardly help recognizing the work of a kindred spirit. Like Sir Willoughby Patterne, he saw his image reflected and found that it was good.

The truth, indeed, is that Browning read a good deal into Wilde's study of Tasso that a disinterested reader cannot find there. To the uninstructed eye, Wilde's method in his two volumes does not seem especially adventurous. Richard Henry Wilde (1789–1847), born in Dublin but arrived in America in 1797, had been an attorney-general of Georgia and had served five terms in Congress before he undertook Italian scholarship during an extended visit abroad from 1835 to 1840 or early in 1841. In addition to his discussion of Tasso, Wilde attempted a treatise upon "The Life and Times of Dante" and another upon "The Italian Lyric Poets." The unfinished manuscripts of the last two works are now in the Library of Congress.[6] The aim and the content of Wilde's *Conjectures and Researches* seem fairly described in *The North American Review* for April, 1842: "Mr. Wilde has endeavoured to make the poet tell his own story, and, from the vast collection of his letters and minor poems, to cull out and piece together those personal allusions and statements, which may throw

---

[6] Wilde also gained some recognition as a poet. His lyric "My life is like the summer rose," published in the *Analectic Magazine* for April, 1819, was set to music by Sidney Lanier. *Hesperia: A Poem* was published posthumously in 1867, edited by his son William Cumming Wilde. See *Dictionary of American Biography*, XX, 206–207, for further details of his life.

light on the principal incidents in his life." [7] Wilde's work is as much a collation of materials as it is an original study. He compiled laboriously from Tasso's critics and biographers, and he translated gracefully and at length from Tasso's verse. He was more interested in presenting the materials upon which a judgment could be formed than he was in impressing his own conclusions upon the reader. Something of his attitude and method can be gathered from his introductory comments:

Various conjectures respecting [the love, madness, and imprisonment of Tasso] have been offered; none, perhaps, entirely satisfactory. The value of those which follow will depend on their probability, and that, again, on the number of incidents collected and compared, and the candor and sagacity employed in their collation.[8]

His voice continues modest throughout the two volumes. He views himself as a collator, and his most characteristic remark is, "Either the thing proves itself, or we should fail to prove it." [9]

In Browning's account, as we have already seen, Wilde takes on another character. For Browning's curious summary given below, the materials are, to be sure, contained in Wilde; but Wilde was concerned only with suggesting that Tasso's love for the Princess of Este was a reality and that Tasso merely feigned madness when his passion was discovered. Wilde did not in any way attempt to interpret Tasso's actions in terms of a "false step" and a deviation from "the right

[7] LIV (1842), 502.
[8] *Conjectures and Researches*, I, 7.
[9] *Ibid.*, II, 268.

way." The moral tone and stress here are entirely Browning's:

> *For Tasso, a few words will say how his first false step was an indiscretion; how, having published love-poetry under a false name, and suffered himself to be suspected its author, he, to avoid the ill-consequences, feigned at the Duke's suggestion, Madness; and how his protracted agony at Saint Anna was but an unremitting attempt to free himself from the effect of this false step without being compelled to reveal the truth, and disavow his whole proceedings since the time of that sad starting-aside from the right way.* (167–175)

Through Browning's remarkable habit of creative reading, Wilde's somewhat discursive and elaborately cautious account of Tasso's life has acquired a central moral theme and a unified plot. It has become a tragedy dealing with a fatal error — a "sad starting-aside" from truth — and Tasso's career from his "first false step" onward has assumed new meaning as a dramatic struggle against the meshes of falsehood.

In quoting as his "text" Wilde's statement that Tasso was not "habitually insincere,"[10] Browning turned an incidental remark into a central theme. He might as logically have preached a very different sermon by taking as his text Wilde's

[10] See lines 145–167 of the Essay. In context, Browning's quotation from Wilde is seen to be merely an argument for the genuineness of Tasso's sentiments in certain lines of his poetry. The sentence immediately following the last one quoted by Browning makes this clear: "At the period when these lines were composed, it is hard to imagine what motive could exist for such a deception; and if the fiction usually attributed to poetry is relied on as a sufficient cause for doubting whatever appears in rhyme, we must reject, as feigned, much that the world has long received as true." Wilde was not attempting to clear Tasso's character, but to authenticate a portion of his own evidence.

comment upon other documents, that a description "false in one point, is probably false in all, and . . . the same deceit once practised, may be suspected wherever there is the same temptation." [11]

It becomes clear that Browning used Wilde, however unconsciously, less as a model than as a stalking-horse. He could follow the example of Wilde's "clever volumes" in shaping his interpretation of Chatterton's life only because he had first remade Wilde's method to his own specifications.

2

In praising Wilde, Browning was actually offering a prospectus of his personal system as a special-pleader. Viewed in this light, his zeal as a disciple and a missionary is understandable. It was not until 1871, with the publication of *Prince Hohenstiel-Schwangau*, that Browning once more expressed himself at any length concerning his theories as a special-pleader. In that poem through the lips of Hohenstiel-Schwangau, and in *Red Cotton Night-Cap Country* two years later in his own person, he again grew confidential. By comparing his statements of theory in the Essay with the statements which he made three decades later in these two poems, and by comparing his practice in the Essay with his practice in his mature works,[12] we can see with some clarity to what extent he made his prose work of 1842 a laboratory trial of his method.

In arguing his brief for Chatterton, Browning makes it

[11] *Conjectures and Researches*, I, 77–78.

[12] For this purpose *Bishop Blougram's Apology* (1855), *Mr. Sludge, "The Medium"* (1864), *Prince Hohenstiel-Schwangau* (1871), and *Red Cotton Night-Cap Country* (1873) will be used.

clear that he is consciously trying out what may be considered the three essentials of his procedure in special-pleading. These will be considered separately in the pages that follow.

a. *The very basis of the Essay is an attempt to reveal the hero's intimate point of view concerning his career, to defend his actions as he must have defended them to himself in the inner recesses of his mind.*

This is also the basis of every study in special-pleading that Browning wrote from the Essay onward. The assumption which guides Browning in his work as a pleader of cases is that the hero is powerless to make his own defense to the world at large. He must either have his inner thoughts interpreted for him by the author, acting as narrator, or he must be allowed to speak in the nearest approach to absolute privacy that the conventions of the dramatic monologue can allow.[13] Browning's self-apologist of the dramatic monologues reveals his intimate view of his career to a single individual, and reveals it under peculiarly favorable circumstances. Bishop Blougram is minded to push chairs back after the wine and speak frankly in the intimacy of his own palace. He reveals his course to a single obscure auditor, who cannot hope to be believed if he repeats one word of what the Bishop tells him. Mr. Sludge proposes to reveal all to a host who has already caught him cheating. He makes his revelation in the privacy of his host's drawing room, with the comforting knowledge that he can later contradict or twist to his own ends whatever Horsefall may choose to divulge of his confession. Hohenstiel-Schwangau finds a pretty and attentive listener who, like

[13] Pompilia, Caponsacchi, and Guido, it is true, speak more publicly, with necessity rather than favorable conditions urging them to self-revealment.

him, has seen better days. He can talk to her in private without fear that she can later use his confidences against him.

Even under the most favorable of conditions, however, the self-apologist finds a statement of his inner view of his life a difficult matter. Hohenstiel-Schwangau exclaims:

> *Alack, one lies oneself*
> *Even in the stating that one's end was truth,*
> *Truth only, if one states as much in words!*
> *Give me the inner chamber of the soul*
> *For obvious easy argument! 't is there*
> *One pits the silent truth against a lie —*
> *. . . But, do your best,*
> *Words have to come: and somehow words deflect*
> *As the best cannon ever rifled will.* (2123–2134)

In his first exercise in special-pleading, and three decades later in *Red Cotton Night-Cap Country*, Browning dispensed with the restrictions of the dramatic monologue. His essential purpose was the same — the enabling his hero to "speak for himself," to counter his own point of view against the world's judgment of him — but in these works Browning, in the capacity of narrator, could proceed more directly to give his hero's thoughts. He could, moreover, explain what he was trying to do. "It is needless for us here to interpose," Browning tells us in the Essay (720–724), "that our whole argument goes, not upon what Chatterton said, but what he did: it is part of our proof to show that all his distress arose out of the impossibility of his saying any thing to the real purpose." And in explaining Chatterton's concealed motives for going to London: "It will, of course, be objected, that Chatterton gave the very reasons for his desire to obtain a release from

Bristol that we have rejected. But he was forced to say something, and what came more plausibly?" (737–740) The basic principle of Browning's procedure as a special-pleader is contained in these two sentences. *In Red Cotton Night-Cap Country*, after many years of practice, Browning stated it even more succinctly:

How substitute thing meant for thing expressed? (2959)

Earlier in the poem, Browning had suggested his manner of answering the question:

"I like these amateurs" — our friend had laughed,
Could he turn what he felt to what he thought,
And, that again, to what he put in words . . .
$$(2833–2835)$$

And later in the poem, Browning elaborates the principle behind his method:

He thought . . .
     (Suppose I should prefer "He said?"
Along with every act — and speech is act —
There go, a multitude impalpable
To ordinary human faculty,
The thoughts which give the act significance.
Who is a poet needs must apprehend
Alike both speech and thoughts which prompt to speak.
Part these, and thought withdraws to poetry:
Speech is reported in the newspaper.)
He said, then, probably no word at all,
But thought as follows — in a minute's space —
One particle of ore beats out such leaf! (3276–3287)

In basing his defense upon the impossibility of Chatterton's "saying any thing to the real purpose" in justification of his actions, in attempting to plead Chatterton's case in terms of what Chatterton intimately thought and felt but could not say for himself, Browning was entering his special province as an artist. With "the point of view," as George Herbert Palmer observed, Browning's "special type of poetry is inherently connected." [14]

b. The second essential of Browning's procedure is closely linked with the first: *Browning explains the whole of his hero's later, superficially complex and ambiguous conduct in terms of a single tendency of his nature that is with him at the beginning of his career.*

To understand Chatterton's "true position," Browning tells us in the Essay, "we must remove much of the colouring which subsequent occurrences imparted to the dim beginnings of his course of deception." (224–226) The typical self-apologist of the dramatic monologues proceeds in like manner, first defining the tendency of his career in its "dim beginnings" and then tracing his later conduct in terms of it. Bishop Blougram prefers to talk in metaphor:

> *Now come, let's backward to the starting-place.*
> *See my way: we're two college friends, suppose.*
> *Prepare together for our voyage, then;*
> *Each note and check the other in his work, —*
> *Here's mine, a bishop's outfit; criticize!*
> *What's wrong? why won't you be a bishop too?*
>
> (144–149)

[14] "Robert Browning," in *Formative Types in English Poetry* (Boston, 1917), p. 307.

The Bishop's aim has been to outfit his cabin for the voyage of life with a view to solid comfort above all else. He traces the whole of his career in terms of his desire from the beginning to be "merely much" and to enjoy the pleasures of an "ideal realized" in mundane luxuries and adulation, in preference to an uncomfortable pursuit of abstract truth.[15] Sludge goes back to his boyhood to show how his tendency to brighten the truth with fable-making became by degrees an ordered system of trickery under the encouragement of his patrons.[16]

But it is Hohenstiel-Schwangau who is most expansive among the self-apologists on this, as on the other points of Browning's procedure:

> *Good! It shall be! Revealment of myself!*
> *But listen, for we must co-operate;*
> *I don't drink tea: permit me the cigar!*

> *First, how to make the matter plain, of course —*
> *What was the law by which I lived. Let's see:*
> *Ay, we must take one instant of my life*
> *Spent sitting by your side in this neat room:*
> *Watch well the way I use it, and don't laugh!*
> *Here's paper on the table, pen and ink:*
> *Give me the soiled bit — not the pretty rose!*
> *See! having sat an hour, I'm rested now,*
> *Therefore want work: and spy no better work*
> *For eye and hand and mind that guides them both,*
> *During this instant, than to draw my pen*
> *From blot One — thus — up, up to blot Two — thus —*
> *Which I at last reach, thus, and here's my line*

[15] See *Bishop Blougram's Apology*, lines 78–85, 301ff.
[16] See above, pp. 67 ff.

Five inches long and tolerably straight:
Better to draw than leave undrawn, I think,
Fitter to do than let alone, I hold,
Though better, fitter, by but one degree.　　(22–41)

In this simple action, so the Prince says, he has illustrated his central tendency from the beginning of his career to his downfall; for his aim has been always to patch, to compromise, to keep things safe:

Make what is absolutely new — I can't,
Mar what is made already well enough —
I won't: but turn to best account the thing
That's half-made — that I can. Two blots, you saw
I knew how to extend into a line
Symmetric on the sheet they blurred before —
Such little act sufficed, this time, such thought. (85–91)

By following this inclination for patching and preserving through the actions that made up his career, the pretty auditress can understand "what meant certain things he did of old" which had greatly puzzled far wiser heads:

— why, you'll find them plain,
This way, not otherwise: I guarantee,
Understand one, you comprehend the rest.　(62–64)

Monsieur Léonce Miranda of *Red Cotton Night-Cap Country or Turf and Towers* (as the full title goes) also possessed a nature that ran to compromise, and it was by compromise that he perished. In Miranda's nature two forces waged irreconcilable conflict — the earthy and illicit love of his mistress, which Browning symbolizes as "turf," and his religious aspirations, which Browning designates as "towers." It

93

is in terms of this conflict that Miranda's conduct is interpreted from his youth to his apparent suicide. Browning as narrator wanted to make sure that the reader would not miss this fact:

> *Keep this same*
> *Notion of outside mound and inside mash,*
> *Towers yet intact round turfy rottenness,*
> *Symbolic partial-ravage, — keep in mind!*
> *Here fortune placed his feet who first of all*
> *Found no incumbrance, till head found . . . But hear!*
>
> (1144–1149)

Returning to the Essay after this view of Browning's mature practice, it is possible to see more clearly how the prose piece of 1842 looked forward to Browning's later work in regard to the second essential of his method. Even in turning from Tasso to Chatterton, Browning makes it plain that he intends to trace the labyrinthine ways of Chatterton's career by a single thread:

> *But before we speak of the corresponding passage in Chatterton's story, something should be premised respecting the characteristic shape his first error took, as induced by the liabilities of that peculiar development of genius of which he was the subject.* (175–179)

Chatterton's first error, we learn, was the comparatively harmless imitating of the work of an earlier period. But Chatterton's peculiar powers of simulating the ancient manner involved him almost at once in more serious deceptions. He was urged on by his patrons, and "at every advance in such a career," Browning tells us, "the impossibility of continuing in the spirit of the outset grows more and more apparent."

(212–214) Poor Chatterton, unable to give all up, could only determine to produce more Ellas and Godwyns. Yet his genius was essentially moral. Though day after day found him more deeply involved, he fought valiantly to regain the ways of Truth.

It is in terms of Chatterton's struggle to reform under the most adverse circumstances and in spite of his peculiar ability to profit by deception that Browning explains the boy poet's conduct in his ambiguous and puzzling career. His dealings with Walpole became "the predetermined last acts of a course of dissimulation he would fain discard for ever — on their success." (507–508) His departure from Bristol is attributed to "this and no other motive — to break through his slavery — at any sacrifice to get back to truth." (734–735) His suicide is explained in terms of this struggle and as its culmination in spiritual triumph. Even in *Hohenstiel-Schwangau* Browning did not proceed more directly to his purpose than in his attempt at "showing that [Chatterton] really made the most gallant and manly effort of which his circumstances allowed to break through the sorry meshes that entangled him." (475–478)

c. The third essential of Browning's procedure as a special-pleader is again but a dimension of the first and basic fact, his espousal of a special point of view: *Browning concentrates each of his studies upon a single important question in the life of his hero.*

The question may be, to use the language of *Sordello*, "One of God's large ones" that is difficult to condense into a period; nevertheless it is a single question that gives point and coherence to the whole monologue or narrative. Inevitably it bears upon the central tendency of the hero's nature, and it is in terms of this central tendency that the answer is elaborated. The question of Bishop Blougram's life is whether he believes or disbelieves, a difficult question that requires a thousand lines of finely balanced exposition in reply. The Bishop defines it thus:

> *Fool or knave?*
> *Why needs a bishop be a fool or knave*
> *When there's a thousand diamond weights between?*
> *So, I enlist them. Your picked twelve, you'll find*
> *Profess themselves indignant, scandalized*
> *At thus being held unable to explain*
> *How a superior man who disbelieves*
> *May not believe as well: that's Schelling's way!*
> *It's through my coming in the tail of time,*
> *Nicking the minute with a happy tact.*
> *Had I been born three hundred years ago*
> *They'd say, "What's strange? Blougram of course believes";*
> *And, seventy years since, "disbelieves of course."*
> *But now, "He may believe; and yet, and yet*
> *"How can he?" All eyes turn with interest.*   (404–418)

Sludge seems equally direct in posing the question of his life:

> *What? If I told you all about the tricks?*
> *Upon my soul! — the whole truth, and nought else,*
> *And how there's been some falsehood . . . ?* (55–57)

But the implied question is how Sludge came to indulge in tricks and cheating, how self-desecration came to be his way of life.

96

Hohenstiel-Schwangau, as we have already seen, at first proposes to attempt an almost all-inclusive subject:

> *Good! It shall be! Revealment of myself!*   (22)

He limits his aim as he proceeds:

> — *I don't say, to that plaguy quadrature*
> *"What the whole man meant, whom you wish*
>   *you knew,"*
> *But, what meant certain things he did of old,*
> *Which puzzled Europe,* — . . .   (59–62)

Nevertheless the solution to the two questions might have been the same, for small and large are meaningless terms when character is the subject. The answer to both questions is to be found in the central tendency of Hohenstiel-Schwangau's actions. This may in turn be found by the proper analysis of any single action — such coherency is revealed in the nature of a man provided one has the truly analytic eye:

> *I guarantee,*
> *Understand one [action], you comprehend the rest.*
> *Rays from all round converge to any point:*
> *Study the point then ere you track the rays!*
> *The size o' the circle's nothing; subdivide*
> *Earth, and earth's smallest grain of mustard-seed,*
> *You count as many parts, small matching large,*
> *If you can use the mind's eye: otherwise,*
> *Material optics, being gross at best,*
> *Prefer the large and leave our mind the small* —
> *And pray how many folk have minds can see?* (63–73)

Here what may at first seem mere casuistry on the part of the Prince is actually in its implications an effective description of

Browning's method of working; for in his handling, a focal point is indeed made but a center for all aspects of his hero's character. Like Tennyson's little flower, Browning's single question, his point of focus, is made to mean far beyond the facts in radial hints and suggestions. In studying the point, he studied all. It is thus that Blougram, Sludge, and Hohenstiel-Schwangau reveal themselves.

It is in like manner that Miranda of *Red Cotton Night-Cap Country* is revealed. The central question with which Browning concerns himself is what led Miranda to leap from his belvedere to dash his brains upon the ground below. Insanity, the villagers believed; but Browning held otherwise. Miranda made his leap, Browning maintained, in the hope that angels might bear him up and thus vouchsafe through a miracle his right to keep both his mistress and his faith. His error was not in his conclusions, but in the premises that others had taught him:

> *No! sane, I say.*
> *Such being the conditions of his life,*
> *Such end of life was not irrational.* (3605–3607)

Nearly twenty-five hundred lines earlier, after a lengthy and discursive introduction, Browning had given the point and theme of his tale:

> *And all at once the climbing landed him*
> *—Where, is my story:*
>   *Take its moral first.*
> *Do you advise a climber? Have respect*
> *To the poor head, with more or less of brains*
> *To spill, should breakage follow your advice!*
>   (1123–1127)

In the interim, he had gone through the whole of Miranda's life. Yet all is told in terms of the one question.

As we have already seen, Browning in 1842 praised Richard Henry Wilde for having "steadily restricted himself to the single point in question" and proposed to follow Wilde in tracing Chatterton's career. In the light of his own later practice, Browning's comments on Wilde's method may be worth reviewing even at the expense of some repetition:

Still it is but a point; and Mr. Wilde has not perhaps done less gracefully and wisely in leaving the rest untouched, than in accomplishing so thoroughly the task he took in hand. He relies upon his subject; is sure of the service he can render by an efficacious treatment of thus much of it; nor entertains any fear lest the bringing in a Before and After, with which he has no immediate concern, should be thought necessary to give interest to the At Present on which he feels he can labour to advantage. We suspect that if we would make any material progress in knowledge of this description, such works must be so undertaken. (91–101)

Here the bias seems more important than the literal statement. Browning as a special-pleader did not in the Essay or in his later work concentrate so completely on the "At Present" that he failed to bring in "a Before and After" to illuminate his immediate subject; but he did direct all his attention to the "single point in question," and that is apparently what he considered new and significant in Wilde's method:

If, for example, the materials for a complete biography of Tasso are far from exhausted, let some other traveller from the west be now busied in the land of Columbus and Vespucci

*with the investigation, — say, of the circumstances of the won-
drous youth of Tasso; the orations at Naples and the Theses
at Padua, — and in the end we should more than probably
have two spots of sunshine to find our way by, instead of one
such breadth of dubious twilight, as, in a hazy book written
on the old principle of doing a little for every part of a subject, and more than a little for none, rarely fails to perplex
the more.* (102–112)

It was by applying this lesson from Wilde that he hoped to
add his own spot of sunshine to Chatterton biography:

*We can show, we think, and by some such process as Mr.
Wilde adopts in regard to Tasso, that [Chatterton] had already entered on those ways when he was left, without a helping hand, to sink and starve as he might. And to this single
point we shall as far as possible restrict ourselves.* (145–149)

And it was this aspect of his own practice that Browning at
the close of the Essay urged others to follow, using his study
of Chatterton as he had used Wilde's volumes.

It is clear that Browning considered his concentration upon
a single question of Chatterton's career the most notable fact
of his method in the Essay, the fact which made his method
capable of substituting solar radiance for the dubious twilight
of earlier writers, which made it worth the study and emula-
tion of other authors.

3

The Essay, then, is a tentative exercise, a laboratory model,
in the process of special-pleading. It possesses the attributes
common to laboratory models. There is a patent self-con-

sciousness on the part of its maker regarding his purposes and his means of effecting them; there is little attempt to round surfaces and conceal the angular machinery that does the work.

This is not to say that the Essay is without literary merit; Browning's Chatterton can claim a place in Browning's memorable gallery of men and women. But the Essay is at least as interesting for what it prophesies as for what it realizes. In this unacknowledged prose work we see clearly for the first time how the essential artist of the 1840's was feeling his way toward *The Ring and the Book* and the great dramatic monologues of his maturity.

❦ II ❦

Essay on Chatterton

The text of *The Foreign Quarterly Review* for July, 1842, is given here except in the following instances, where obvious errors are corrected:

Line 239   *Mayors* altered to read *Mayor's*.

"   314   βαπτιζετα altered to read βαπτιζεται.

"   459   *ballad* capitalized.

"   459   quotation marks inserted after *face*.

"   764   *Thistlewaites* altered to read *Thistlethwaites*.

"   767   quotation marks inserted before *knowing*.

"   845   *tergiversification* altered to read *tergiversation*.

"   872   *must not not stay* altered to read *must not stay*.

ART. VIII. — *Conjectures and Researches concerning the Love Madness and Imprisonment of Torquato Tasso.* By RICHARD HENRY WILDE. 2 vols. New York. 1842.

UPON the minuteness and obscurity of our attainable evidences with regard to a single important portion of a great poet's history — the Love and Madness of Tasso — great light is thrown by these clever volumes. And further additions to a very meagre stock are not, it seems, to be absolutely 5 despaired of. The Medicean Records may be laid under more liberal contributions, and the Archives of Este cease to remain impenetrable. What even if a ray of light should straggle over the unsunned hoards of sumless wealth in the Vatican? "If windows were in heaven, might this thing be." 10

But in our days the poorest loophole will have to be broken, we suspect, with far different instruments from those it is the fashion to employ just now in Italy. It is enough at present if the oily instances of this or the other Minister-Residentiary operate so happily upon the ruffled apprehen- 15 siveness of this or the other Chamberlain-Omnipotentiary, as to allow a minute's glimpse of the Fortunate Isles through the incessant breakers that girdle them. The rude sea now and then grows civil, indeed; but a positive current setting landwards is the thing wanted, and likely to remain so. Ever 20 and anon we seem on the point of a discovery. A scrap of letter turns up, or a bundle of notices drop out, and the Head Librarian for the time being considers the curiosity of some Dilettante Ambassador for the place being, and, provided the interest of the whole civilized world is kept out of sight with sufficient adroitness, becomes communicative.

"The anger of the Grand Duke arises from his being informed that I had revealed to the Duke of Ferrara . . . . . . ! I cannot write all freely, but this is the gospel." So writes Tasso to "the one friend he now believes in, Scipio Gonzaga." And "this blank," sorrowfully subjoins Mr. Wilde, "is found in the first copy of the letter furnished for publication by the learned and candid Muratori, then librarian to the Duke of Modena." It contained an expression, says he, which it would be indecorous to repeat! Thus at every step, where there is the slightest prospect of a clue to the truth, are we mortified by its destruction through reserve or timidity. And if things were so in the green-tree time of the Muratoris, what shall be done in the dry stump of modern Lombardy or Tuscany?

Of certain important manuscripts recently discovered at Rome, and now in the course of publication, we regret to learn that the authenticity is considered too questionable to allow of their being brought forward to any useful purpose: so that, for the present, this result of Mr. Wilde's labour, now before us, must be regarded as conclusive: and fortunately our last, proves also our best, news. It is pleasant to find that the popular notion (we might say instinct) concerning this particular point of Tasso's career, grown up, uncertain how, from biographical gleanings here and gatherings there, — somewhat shaken, as it was sure to be, by subsequent representations, — seems again confirmed by these latest discoveries.

A couplet in a canzone, a paragraph in an epistle, had thus been sufficient to begin with. "Tasso was punished in a living hell by angels, because he unburthened his bosom to his lyre." "He would fain be released from this prison of Saint Anna

without being troubled for those things which from frenzy
he has done and written in matters of love." After these, and
a few other like notices, Professors might search, and Abbates
research; the single Leonora become "three lady-loves at
once;" and the dim torture at Ferrara a merciful effect of 60
Duke Alfonso's consideration for "Signor Tasso, the noted
poet's, deplorable madness;" — but the world, satisfied with
its own suspicion, remained deaf to it all.

"If we suppose," sums up Mr. Wilde, "that his imprisonment was
occasioned by the accidental or treacherous disclosure of amatory poetry 65
suspected to be addressed to the princess, every thing becomes intelligible
— his mistress's early injunctions of silence — his directions to Rondi-
nelli — the dearer mysteries of his heart half-hinted to Gonzaga — the
reference to her who corresponded so little to his love — his heavy sin
of temerity — Madalò's more important treasons — the attempt to ex- 70
tort confession — the bitter rigour and unwonted arts — the words and
acts that might increase Alfonso's ire — the order to feign insanity —
the sacrifice of Abraham — the command that he must aspire to no
fame of letters — the prohibition to write — the anger of the princesses
— the allusions to his fond faults — to his Proserpine — to Ixion, and 75
to the angels that punished him. By this supposition, also, Leonora's
voluntary celibacy, notwithstanding the most advantageous offers of
marriage, and Tasso's constant devotion to the duke, in spite of the
rigour of his chastisement, are sufficiently accounted for." *

How much that establishes old convictions, and how little that 80
is even supplementary to them, have we here!

Such as it is, however, in what Mr. Wilde has done, he has
gone the right way to work and done it well. He has steadily
restricted himself to the single point in question. It is that
point in the poet's history, indeed, from which those to whom 85
sonnets and madrigals, the Rinaldo and the Aminta, are all

* Vol. II., p. 166.

but unknown, will take warrant for some belief in their reported truth and beauty. It is undoubtedly that to which every student of Italian verse must refer the touching glimmer, as an outbreak through prison-bars, that colours every 90 page of the Giurusalemme. Still it is but a point; and Mr. Wilde has not perhaps done less gracefully and wisely in leaving the rest untouched, than in accomplishing so thoroughly the task he took in hand. He relies upon his subject; is sure of the service he can render by an efficacious treatment 95 of thus much of it; nor entertains any fear lest the bringing in a Before and After, with which he has no immediate concern, should be thought necessary to give interest to the At Present on which he feels he can labour to advantage. We suspect that if we would make any material progress in knowl- 100 edge of this description, such works must be so undertaken. If, for example, the materials for a complete biography of Tasso are far from exhausted, let some other traveller from the west be now busied in the land of Columbus and Vespucci with the investigation, — say, of the circumstances of the won- 105 drous youth of Tasso; the orations at Naples and the Theses at Padua, — and in the end we should more than probably have two spots of sunshine to find our way by, instead of one such breadth of dubious twilight, as, in a hazy book written on the old principle of doing a little for every part of a subject, 110 and more than a little for none, rarely fails to perplex the more.

Thinking thus, and grieving over what must be admitted to be the scantiness of the piece of sunshine here, and the narrow and not very novel track it would alone serve to lead us 115 into, — a book * was sent to us on a subject not very different

* "The Poetical Works of Thomas Chatterton, with Notices of his Life, a

from Mr. Wilde's, but on which the service he has sought to render to the memory of Tasso has not hitherto been attempted for a memory more foully outraged. We make no apology for a proposed effort to render some such service. It is no very abrupt desertion of the misfortunes of Tasso, to turn to the misfortunes of Chatterton. All these disputed questions in the lives of men of genius — all these so-called calamities of authors — have a common relationship, a connexion so close and inalienable, that they seldom fail to throw important light upon each other.

To the precocity of genius in the Neapolitan boy at seven years old — the verse and prose from the College of the Jesuits — no parallel can be found in modern times, till we arrive at the verses of Chatterton, to whom Campbell has very properly said "Tasso alone may be compared as a juvenile prodigy." But the parallel will, in other respects, admit of application. The book before us, for example, on the love and madness of the Italian, is in itself a direct text from which to speak of what concerns us most in the disputed character of our own countryman. As the whole of Mr. Wilde's argument may be said to include itself in his commentary upon the opening couplet of the first Sonnet of the collection of *Rime*,

"True were the loves and transports which I sung,"

so let us say of the Englishman, that his were far from that untruth, that absence of reality, so constantly charged against them. In a word, poor Chatterton's life was not the Lie it is so universally supposed to have been; nor did he "perish in the pride" of refusing to surrender Falsehood and enter on the

---

History of the Rowley Controversy, a Selection of his Letters, and Notes Critical and Explanatory." Cambridge. 1842.

ways of Truth. We can show, we think, and by some such 145
process as Mr. Wilde adopts in regard to Tasso, that he had
already entered on those ways when he was left, without a
helping hand, to sink and starve as he might. And to this
single point we shall as far as possible restrict ourselves.

Mr. Wilde remarks of the great Italian, that though there 150
are indeed passages in Tasso's life and letters, scarcely recon-
cilable with the strict regard for truth which Manso, his friend
and contemporary, ascribes to him,

"yet that to whatever dissimulation he may have been driven, upon some
memorable occasions — by a hard and, if you will, a criminal, but still 155
almost irresistible necessity — there is no reason to believe him habitually insincere: and that, avoiding every subtle refinement, it cannot be
too much to assume that he was like other men, who in the absence of
all inducement, were not supposed deliberately to utter falsehood." *

It shall be our endeavour, by extending the application of this 160
text from Tasso to Chatterton, to throw a new light upon a
not dissimilar portion of the latter poet's career, and in some
degree soften those imputations of habitual insincerity with
which the most sympathizing of Chatterton's critics have
found themselves compelled to replace the "great veracity" 165
attributed to him by his earliest and most partial biographer.

For Tasso, a few words will say how his first false step was
an indiscretion; how, having published love-poetry under a
false name, and suffered himself to be suspected its author,
he, to avoid the ill-consequences, feigned at the Duke's sugges- 170
tion, Madness; and how his protracted agony at Saint Anna
was but an unremitting attempt to free himself from the effect
of this false step without being compelled to reveal the truth,
and disavow his whole proceedings since the time of that sad

* Vol. I., p. 12.

starting-aside from the right way. But before we speak of the 175
corresponding passage in Chatterton's story, something
should be premised respecting the characteristic shape his first
error took, as induced by the liabilities of that peculiar development of genius of which he was the subject.

Genius almost invariably begins to develop itself by imita- 180
tion. It has, in the short-sightedness of infancy, faith in the
world: and its object is to compete with, or prove superior to,
the world's already recognised idols, at their own perfor-
mances and by their own methods. This done, there grows up
a faith in itself: and, no longer taking the performance or 185
method of another for granted, it supersedes these by processes of its own. It creates, and imitates no longer. Seeing
cause for faith in something external and better, and having
attained to a moral end and aim, it next discovers in itself the
only remaining antagonist worthy of its ambition, and in the 190
subduing what at first had seemed its most enviable powers,
arrives at the more or less complete fulfilment of its earthly
mission. This first instinct of Imitation, which with the mediocre takes the corresponding mediocre form of an implied
rather than expressed appropriation of some other man's 195
products, assumed perforce with Chatterton, whose capabilities were of the highest class, a proportionably bolder and
broader shape in the direction his genius had chosen to take.
And this consideration should have checked the too severe
judgment of what followed. For, in simple truth, the start- 200
ling character of Chatterton's presentment, with all its strange
and elaborately got up accompaniments, was in no more than
strict keeping with that of the thing he presented. For one
whose boy's essay was "Rowley" (a Man, a Time, a Language, all at once) the simultaneous essay of inventing the 205

details of muniment-room treasures and yellow-roll discoveries, by no means exceeded in relative hardihood the mildest possible annexing — whatever the modern author's name may be — to the current poetry or prose of the time. But, alas! for the mere complacent forbearance of the world in the one case, must come sharp and importunate questionings in the other; and, at every advance in such a career, the impossibility of continuing in the spirit of the outset grows more and more apparent. To begin with the step of a giant is one thing, suddenly for another's satisfaction to increase to a colossal stride is a very different. To the falsehood of the mediocre, truth may easily be superinduced, and true works, with them, silently take the place of false works: but before one like Chatterton could extricate himself from the worse than St. Anna dungeon which every hour was building up more surely between him and the common earth and skies, so much was to be dared and done! That the attempt was courageously made in Chatterton's case, there are many reasons for believing. But to understand his true position, we must remove much of the colouring which subsequent occurrences imparted to the dim beginnings of his course of deception. He is to the present day viewed as a kind of Psalmanazar or Macpherson, producing deliberately his fabrications to the world and challenging its attention to them. A view far from the truth. Poor Chatterton never had that chance. Before the world could be appealed to, a few untoward circumstances seem to have effectually determined and given stability to what else had not impossibly proved a mere boy's fancy, destined to go as lightly as it came and leave no trace, save in a fresh exertion of the old means to a new and more commensurate end.

In September, 1768, a New Bridge at Bristol was completed, and early in the next month the principal newspaper of the city contained a prose "description of the Fryar's (Mayor's) first passing over the Old Bridge, taken from an old manuscript." The attention of — what are called in the accounts we have seen — "the literati of Bristol," was excited. Application was made to the publisher for a sight of the surprising and interesting original. No such thing was forthcoming; but the curiosity of Literati must be appeased; and the bearer of the newspaper marvel, one Thomas Chatterton, — a youth of sixteen, educated at Colston's Charity-school where reading, writing and arithmetic only were taught, and, since, a clerk to an attorney of the place, — was recognised on his next appearance at the printing-office with another contribution, and questioned whence he obtained that first-named paper. He was questioned "with threatenings in the first instance, to which he refused any answer, and next with milder usage and promises of patronage," — which extorted from him at last the confession, that the manuscript was one of many his father (parish clerk, usher, or sexton) had taken from a coffer in the church of St. Mary, Redcliff.

It was his own composition; and being the first of what are called the Rowleian forgeries, suggests a remark upon literary forgery in general, and that of Chatterton in particular.*

* [BROWNING'S NOTE] That there should have been a controversy for ten minutes about the genuineness of any ten verses of "Rowley" is a real disgrace to the scholarship of the age in which such a thing took place: we shall not touch on it here, certainly. Conceive the entering on such a discussion at all, when the poor charity-boy had himself already furnished samples of Rowley in the different stages of partial completeness, from the rough draught in the English of the day, ungarnished by a single obsolete word, to the finished piece with its strange incrustation of antiquity! There is never theft for theft's sake with

Chatterton. One short poem only, *The Romaunt of the Cnyghte*, is in
part a tacking together of old lines from old poets, out of rhyme and 270
time, yet at the same time not so utterly unlike an approximation to the
genuine ware. And why? Because the Mr. Burgum, to one of whose
ancestors it is attributed, and whose taste solely it was intended to suit,
happened to be *hopelessly incapable of understanding any composition
of the mixed sort which Chatterton had determined upon producing;* 275
*and which, retaining what he supposed the ancient garb should also
include every modern refinement.* The expedient which would alone
serve with the good Mr. Burgum, was to ply him with something entirely unintelligible, so begetting a reverence; and after that with another thing perfectly comprehensible, so ministering to his pleasure. 280
Accordingly, Chatterton, for that once, attempted to write thorough old
verse, because he could, as he did, accompany it by thorough new verse
too: a modern paraphrase to wit.

But though we will not touch the general and most needless question,
it happens that, by a curious piece of fortune, we have been enabled, 285
since taking up the subject of this article, to bring home to Chatterton
one, and by no means the least ingenious of his "forgeries," which has
hitherto escaped detection. Rowley's *Sermon on the Holy Spirit*, with
its orthodoxy and scripture citations, its Latin from St. Cyprian, and its
Greek from St. Gregory, is triumphantly referred to by the learned and 290
laborious Jacob Bryant (who wrote one folio to disprove the Tale of
Troy and another to prove the Tale of Rowley), as a flight clearly above
Chatterton's reach. Now this aforesaid Greek quotation was the single
paragraph which struck our eye some two or three days since, in looking
hastily through a series of sermons on the Nature of the Holy Spirit, 295
by the Rev. John Hurrion, originally printed, it should seem, in 1732;
on a reference to which we found Rowley's discourse to be a mere cento
from their pages, artfully enough compiled. For example, thus saith
Rowley: "Seyncte Paulle prayethe the Holye Spryte toe assyste hys
flocke ynn these wordes, The Holye Spryte's communyonn bee wythe 300
you. Lette us dhere desyerr of hymm to ayde us . . . lette us saye
wythe Seyncte Cyprian, '*Adesto, Sancte Spiritus, et paraclesin tuam
expectantibus illabere cœlitus; sanctifica templum corporis nostri et consecra inhabitaculum tuum.*' Seyncte Paulle sayethe yee are the temple

114

of Godde; for the Spryte of Godde dwellethe ynn you. Gyff yee are 305
the temple of Godde alleyne bie the dwellynge of the Spryte, wote yee
notte that the Spryte ys Godde? . . . The Spryte or dyvyne will of
Godde moovedd uponn the waterrs att the Creatyonn of the worlde;
thys meaneth the Deeitie . . . . Gyff the Spryte bee notte Godde,
howe bee ytt the posessynge of the Spryte dothe make a manne sayedd 310
toe be borne of Godde? Itt requyreth the powerr of Godde toe make
a manne a new creatyonn, yette such dothe the Spryte. Thus sayethe
Seyncte Gregorie Naz. of the Spryte and hys wurchys: Γενᾶται Χριστος·
προτρέχει. βαπτιζεται· μαρτυρεῖ. Πειραζέται· αναγεῖ. Δυναμεις ἐπιτελεῖ·
ξυμπαραμαρτεῖ. Ανέρχεται." And now let us listen to Hurrion, Serm. 1. 315
"As therefore the apostle prayed on the behalf of the Corinthians . . . .
in these words: 'The communion of the Holy Ghost be with you,' it is
very proper to apply to him for his gracious aid and assistance. An example of this we have in Cyprian. 'O Holy Spirit be thou present,' &c. —
Cyp. de Spir. S. p. 484. [quoted, no doubt, at length, like the other 320
references, in the first edition.] . . . . Now if he that dwells in us
as his temple is God, what other conclusion can be drawn from thence
but this, that we are the temple of God? &c. &c. [The rest of the verse,
with the authority of St. Paul being the text of the Sermon.] . . . .
which is also God — as when it is said 'the Spirit of God moved upon 325
the waters, in the creation of the world. Sermon 4. Believers are born
of the Spirit . . this is a new creation, and requires the same Almighty
power to effect as the first creation did . . if the Spirit is not God by
nature . . how are they said to be born of God who are regenerated
by the Spirit? 'Christ,' says one of the ancients, 'is born — the Spirit is 330
his forerunner,' &c." And in a foot-note the Greek text and proper
authority are subjoined.

It is, perhaps, worth a remark in concluding this note, that Chatterton, a lawyer's clerk, takes care to find no law-papers in Canning's
Coffer, of which tradition had declared it to be full. That way detection 335
was to be feared. But the pieces on devotional subjects, to which his
earlier taste inclined, came so profusely from the "Godlie preeste Rowlie," that Chatterton thinks it advisable, from the time of his discoveries,
to forget his paraphrases of Job and Isaiah, and to disclaim for himself
a belief in Christianity on every and no occasion at all! 340

Is it worth while to mention, that the very notion of obtaining a free way for impulses that can find vent in no other
channel (and consequently of a liberty conceded to an individual, and denied to the world at large), is implied in all literary production? By this fact is explained, not only the pop- 345
ular reverence for, and interest in even the personal history of,
the acknowledged and indisputable possessors of this power —
as so many men who have leave to do what the rest of their
fellows cannot — but also the as popular jealousy of allowing
this privilege to the first claimant. And so instinctively does 350
the Young Poet feel that his desire for this kind of self-
enfranchisement will be resisted as a matter of course, that we
will venture to say, in nine cases out of ten his first assumption
of the licence will be made in a borrowed name. The first communication, to even the family circle or the trusted associate, 355
is sure to be "the work of a friend;" if not, "something ex-
tracted from a magazine," or "Englished from the German."
So is the way gracefully facilitated for Reader and Hearer
finding themselves in a new position with respect to each
other.   360

Now unluckily, in Chatterton's case, this communication's
whole value, in the eyes of the Bristolians, consisted in its
antiquity. Apart from that, there was to them no picturesque-
ness in "Master Mayor, mounted on a white horse, dight with
sable trappings wrought about by the nuns of St. Kenna;" no 365
"most goodly show in the priests and freres all in white albs."
Give that up, and all was given; and poor Chatterton could
not give all up. He could only determine for the future to
produce Ellas and Godwyns, and other "beauteous pieces;"
wherein "the plot should be clear, the language spirited; and 370
the songs interspersed in it, flowing, poetical, and elegantly

simple; the similes judiciously applied; and though written in the reign of Henry VI., not inferior to many of the present age." Had there but been any merit of this kind, palpable even to Bristol Literati, to fall back upon in the first instance, 375 if the true authorship were confessed! But that was otherwise; and so the false course, as we have said, was unforeseeingly entered upon. Yet still, from the first, he was singularly disposed to become communicative of his projects and contrivances for carrying them into effect. There was, after all, 380 no such elaborate deception about any of them. Indeed, had there only happened to be a single individual of ordinary intelligence among his intimates, the event must assuredly have fallen out differently. But as it was, one companion would be present at the whole process of "antiquating," as 385 Chatterton styled it, his productions (the pounding of ochre and crumpling of parchments); another would hear him carelessly avow himself master of a power "to copy, by the help of books he could name, the style of our elder poets so exactly, that they should escape the detection of Mr. Walpole him- 390 self;" — and yet both these persons remain utterly incapable of perceiving that such circumstances had in the slightest degree a bearing upon after events at Bristol! It is to be recollected, too, that really in Bristol itself there was not any thing like a general interest excited in the matter. And when 395 at last, yielding to the pertinacity of inquirers, these and similar facts came lingeringly forth, as the details of so many natural appearances with which unconscious rustics might furnish the philosopher anxious to report and reason upon them — Chatterton was dead. 400

Of several of his most characteristic compositions, he confessed, at various times, on the least solicitation, the authorship. He had found and versified the argument of the Bristowe Tragedy — he had written the Lines on our Ladye's Church. But these confidences were only to his mother and 405 sister. Why? Because mother and sister were all who cared for him rather than for Rowley, and would look at his connexion with any verses as a point in their favour. As for his two patrons, Barrett and Catcott, they took great interest in the yellow streaks, and verse written like prose without stops; 410 less interest in the poetry; and in Chatterton least, or none at all! And a prophet's fate in his own country was never more amusingly exemplified than when grave Deans and Doctors, writing to inquire after Chatterton's abilities of his old companions, got the answers on record. "Not having any 415 taste myself for ancient poetry," writes Mr. Cary, "I do not recollect Chatterton's ever having shown such writings to me, *but* he often mentioned them, *when*, great as his capacity was, I am convinced that he was incapable of writing them!" "He had intimated," remarks Mr. Smith, "very frequently both a 420 desire to learn, and a design to teach himself — Latin; but I always dissuaded him from it, *as being in itself impracticable.* But I advised him by all means *to try* at French. As to Latin, *depend upon it you will find it too hard for you.* Try at French, if you please: of *that* you may acquire *some* knowl- 425 edge *without much difficulty*, and it will be of real service to you." "And, sir," winds up Mr. Clayfield, "*take my word for it*, the poems were no more his composition than *mine*!" With such as these there was no fellowship possible for Chatterton. We soon discover him, therefore, looking beyond. 430 From the time of his communication of the Rowley poems, "his ambition," writes Mrs. Newton, his sister, "increased daily. When in spirits he would enjoy his rising fame; confi-

dent of advancement, he would promise that my mother and I
should be partakers of his success." As a transcriber, we 435
suppose! We find Sir Herbert Croft, to whom this very letter
was addressed, declaring "that he will not be sure that the
writer and her mother might not have easily been made to
believe that injured justice demanded their lives at Tyburn,
for being the relatives of him who forged the poems of 440
Rowley." Thus only, in this sideway at the best, could the
truth steal out.

Meanwhile the sorry reception given to the so-called falsehood produced its natural effects. On the one hand there is a
kind of ambition on being introduced to Mr. Barrett and Mr. 445
Catcott, which increases daily; but on the other we are told
that his spirits became at the same time "rather uneven —
sometimes so *gloomed*,* that for some days together he would
say very little, and that by constraint." No doubt, and no
wonder! For there was the sense of his being the author of 450
the transcendent chorus to Freedom, or the delicious roundelay in Ella; ever at fierce variance with the pitiful claim he
was entitled to make in the character of their mere transcriber.

* [Browning's Note] The only word in Chatterton's communication to the genuineness of which Walpole seems to have objected. "The 455
modern gloomy," says Chatterton, in reply to some critical exception
taken against poems he had sent, "seems but a refinement of the old
word Glomming, in Anglo-Saxon the twilight." And in a note to a
line of the Ballad of Charity, "Look in his *glommed* face," &c., he ob-
serves, " 'Glommed' clouded, dejected. A person of some note in the 460
literary world is of opinion that 'glum' and 'glom' are modern cant
words, and from this circumstance doubts the authenticity of Rowley
MSS. 'Glummong,' in the Saxon signifies twilight, a dark or dubious
light and the modern word gloomy is derived from the Saxon 'glum.' "
It is to be added that Chatterton, throughout, only objects to men's 465

doubting the genuineness of Rowley on the insufficient grounds they give — and is in the right there.

We shall not pursue this painful part of the question. Day followed day, and found him only more and more deeply involved. What we have restricted our inquiry to, is the justice 470 or injustice of the common charge that henceforth the whole nature of Chatterton became no other than one headstrong spirit of Falsehood, in the midst of which, and by which, he perished at the last. And we think its injustice will be shown without much difficulty, in showing that he really made the 475 most gallant and manly effort of which his circumstances allowed to break through the sorry meshes that entangled him. We purposely forbear, with any view to this, taking for granted the mere instigation of that Moral Sense which it is the worst want of charity to deny to him, and with direct and 480 strong evidences of which his earliest poetry abounded. We will simply inquire what, in the circumstances referred to, would have been the proper course to pursue, had the writer of the "Bristowe Tragedy" chanced to adopt on a single occasion the practice of its hero, "who summed the actions of the 485 day each night before he slept." Confessions at the market-cross avail nothing, and most injure those to whom they are unavoidably made. Should he not have resolutely left Bristol, at least? and, disengaging himself from the still increasing trammels of his daily life of enforced deceit, begun elsewhere 490 a wiser and happier course? That he did so may in our opinion be shown. It is our firm belief that on this, and no other account, he determined to go to London.

"A few months before he left Bristol," mentions his sister, "he wrote letters to several booksellers in London — I be- 495 lieve to learn if there was any probability of his getting an employment there." He had some time previously applied to Dodsley, the noted publisher, for his assistance in printing the tragedy of *Ella*; on the strength of a submitted specimen, which the great man of the Mall did not vouchsafe, it seems, to glance over. He was led, therefore, to make a final experiment on the taste and apprehensiveness of Horace Walpole: not, as in Dodsley's case, by enclosing the despised poetical samples, but by sending a piece of antiquarian ware in which his presumed patron was understood to especially delight. Of nothing are we so thoroughly persuaded as that these attempts were the predetermined last acts of a course of dissimulation he would fain discard for ever — on their success. The Rowleian compositions were all he could immediately refer to, as a proof of the ability he was desirous of employing in almost any other direction. He grounded no claim on his possession of these MSS.; he was not soliciting an opportunity of putting off to advantage the stock in hand, or increasing it; and when Walpole subsequently avowed his regret at having omitted to transcribe before returning, the manuscript thus received, what has been cited as a singular piece of unprincipled effrontery, appears to us perfectly justifiable. For even after the arrival of a discouraging letter, Chatterton's words are, that "if Mr. Walpole wishes to publish them himself, they are at his service." Nay — Mr. Barrett, or "the Town and Country Magazine, to which copies may be sent," or indeed "the world, which it would be the greatest injustice to deprive of so invaluable a curiosity" — may have them and welcome. And Chatterton's anxiety to recover them afterwards is only intelligible on the supposition that his originals were in jeopardy. To the very conceited question Walpole himself has asked — "Did Chatterton impute to me anything but distrust

500

505

510

515

520

525

of his MSS.?" — we should answer, Every thing but that. Let the young poet's own verses, indeed, answer.

> Walpole, I thought not I should ever see 530
> So mean a heart as thine has proved to be:
> Thou, who in luxury nursed, behold'st with scorn
> The boy who friendless, fatherless, forlorn,
> Asks thy high favour. *Thou mayst call me cheat —*
> *Say didst thou never practise such deceit?* 535
> *Who wrote Otranto?* — but I will not chide.
> Scorn I'll repay with scorn, and pride with pride.
> Had I the gifts of wealth and luxury shared —
> Not poor and mean — Walpole! thou hadst not dared
> Thus to insult. But I shall live and stand 540
> By Rowley's side, when thou art dead and damned.

In this unhappy correspondence with Walpole, — it never seems to have been admitted, yet it cannot be said too often, — there is no new "falsehood" discernible: there is nothing but an unavailing and most affecting effort, to get somehow free 545 from the old. He makes no asseveration of the fact of his discoveries; affirms nothing the denial of which hereafter would be essentially disgraceful to him; commits himself by only a few ambiguous words which at any time a little plain speaking (and blushes, if we will) would explain away. Let it be ob- 550 served, above all, that there is no attempt to forge, and produce, and insist on the genuineness of the MSS.; though this was a step by which he could have lost nothing and might have gained every thing, since Walpole's recognition of their extraordinary merit was before him. In the course the corre- 555 spondence took, alas! that very recognition was fatal. If Walpole could suspect a boy of sixteen had written thus, and yet see nothing in a scrivener's office and its duties which such an one had any title to withdraw from, all was over with Chatterton's hopes. At this point, accordingly, he simply replied that, 560 "he is not able to dispute with a person of his literary character: he has transcribed Rowley's poems from a transcript in the possession of a gentleman who is assured of their authenticity," (poor Catcott!) "and he will go a little beyond Walpole's advice, by destroying *all his useless lumber of literature* 565 *and never urging his pen again but in the law.*" Is this any very close or deliberate keeping of Rowley's secret! In a word, he felt that Walpole should have said, "Because I firmly believe you, Chatterton, wrote or forged these verses of Rowley, I will do what you require." * And so we all feel 570 now.

* [BROWNING'S NOTE] Walpole's share in the matter may be told in a few words. Indifferent antiquary as he was, at best — in these matters, at worst, his ignorance was complete. "The admirable reasoning in Bryant's work" could "stagger him," he confesses. On receiving Chat- 575 terton's first letter and specimens, as his belief in them was implicit, so his mortification on Gray and Mason's setting him right was proportionable. "They both pronounced the poems to be modern forgeries, and recommended the returning them without any further notice," — stepping a little out of their province in that, certainly; *but they might* 580 *have felt Chatterton safer at Bristol than nearer home.* Walpole himself did no more in the refusal he gave, than avail himself of Chatterton's own statement that his communications were "taken from a transcript in the possession of a gentleman who was assured of their authenticity." This unknown personage had clearly the first claim to the good things 585 of the Clerk of the Pipe and Usher of the Receipt, and to the unknown they were left therefore, without more heed. Who can object? Truth to say, he of Strawberry Hill was at all times less disposed to expend his doit on a living beggar than on a dead Indian; and, in his way, cowls-full of Ellas and Godwyns were nothing to a spurious cardinal's hat, 590 empty enough. Beside, what was there to him in the least pressing in

the application of a mere transcriber ("who had not quitted his master, nor was necessitous, nor otherwise poorer than attorney's clerks are"), to "emerge from a dull profession and obtain a place that would enable him to follow his propensities." Therefore is it more a pity that ten 595 years after, when he had partly forgotten the matter (this must be allowed, since, with respect to two points which strengthen his case materially, he professes uncertainty), Walpole should have made, on compulsion, a statement of its main circumstances, and leisurely put himself in what he conceived the handsomest of positions, — which 600 turns out to be not quite so handsome. Never for an instant, forsooth, was he deceived by Rowley. "Chatterton had not commenced their intercourse in a manner to dazzle his judgment, or give him a high idea of Chatterton's own." "Somebody, he at first supposed, desired to laugh at him, not very ingeniously, he thought." Little imagining 605 all this while that his letters were in existence, and forthcoming! and that every piece of encouragement to further forgeries, by the expression of belief in those before him, which he professes would have been the height of baseness in him to make, *he had already made!* Indeed the whole statement is modelled on Benedick's *Old Tale:* "If this were 610 so, so were it uttered — but it is not so, nor 'twas not so — but, indeed, God forbid it should be so!" One while, he "does not believe there ever existed so masterly a genius as Chatterton." And another while, he has regard to the "sad situation of the world, if every muse-struck lad who is bound to an attorney were to have his fetters struck off." Wanting 615 is the excellent Horace Walpole, in short, through all these unhappy matters, in that good memory which Swift has pronounced indispensable to a certain class of statement-makers.

And here would enough seem to have been said on the subject, did not one vile paragraph in the Walpole Explanations leer at us — the 620 news to wit, that "all of the house of forgery are relations, and that Chatterton's ingenuity in counterfeiting styles, and it is believed, hands, might easily have led him to those more facile imitations of prose, promissory notes." House of forgery! — from one not only enabled by his first preface to Otranto to march in at its hall-door, but qualified, by a 625 trait noted in "Walpoliana," to sneak in through its area-wicket! *Exempli gratiâ*. "The compiler having learned that the celebrated epistle

to Sir William Chambers was supposed to be written by Mason, very
innocently expressed to Mr. Walpole his surprise that Mason, the general
characteristic of whose poesy is feeble delicacy, but united with a pleasing 630
neatness, should be capable of composing so spirited a satire. Mr. Walpole, *with an arch and peculiar smile, answered, that it would indeed
be surprising.* An instantaneous and unaccountable impression arose that
he was himself the author, but delicacy prevented the direct question,"
&c. &c. 635

And what was it the poor baffled youth required? To ascertain this will in a manner satisfy our whole inquiry — so let us
try to ascertain it. His immediate application to Walpole, on
his succeeding in forcing his notice, and seemingly engaging
his interest, was for some place in a government-office. Did 640
he want to be richer? who had from his earliest boyhood been
accustomed to live upon bread and water, and who would refuse to partake of his mother's occasional luxury of a hot meal,
— remarking that "he was about a great work, and must make
himself no stupider than God had made him." Did he want to 645
obtain leisure, then, for this work — in other words, for the
carrying on of his old deceptions? "He had," says his sister,
"little of his master's business to do — sometimes not two
hours in a day, which gave him an opportunity to pursue his
genius." Mr. Palmer states, that "Chatterton was much alone 650
in his office, and much disliked being disturbed in the day-
time." We should like to know what kind of government-
office would have allowed greater facility for the pursuit of
poetical studies and "forgeries" than he was already in possession of; since what advantages, in a literary life, government- 655
office-labour can have over law-business, we are far from
guessing. It may be said that the pure disgust and weariness
of that law business had formed motive sufficient. But our

sympathy with Chatterton's struggles — were nothing to be escaped from worse than this "servitude" as he styles it — would seriously diminish, we confess. Relieve Henry Jones from the bricklayer's hod, and Stephen Duck from the thrasher's flail, if needs must: but Chatterton, from two hours a day's copying precedents! — Ay, but "he was obliged to sleep in the same room with the footboy, and take his meals with the servants — which degradation, to one possessing such pride as Chatterton, must have been mortifying in the highest degree!" Now, Chatterton taking his stand on the inherent qualities of his own mind, shall part company with an Emperor, if he so please, and have our approbation; but let him waive that prerogative, and condescend to the little rules of little men, and we shall not sufficiently understand this right — in a blue-coat charity-boy, apprenticed out with ten pounds of the school-fund, and looking for patronage to pipe-makers and pewterers — to cherish this sensitiveness of contamination. There are more degrading things than eating with foot-boys, we imagine. "The desire," for example, "of proving oneself worthy the correspondence of Mr. Stephens (leather breeches-maker of Salisbury), by tracing his family from Fitz Stephen, son of Stephen, Earl of Aumerle, in 1095, son of Od, Earl of Bloys, and Lord of Holderness." In a word, Chatterton was very proud, and such crotchets never yet entered the head of a truly proud man. Another motive remains. Had he any dislike to Bristol or its inhabitants generally? "His company pleased universally," he says: "he believed he had promised to write to some hundreds of his acquaintance." And for the place itself, — while at London, nothing out of the Gothic takes his taste, except St. Paul's and Greenwich-hospital: he is never tired of talking in his letters about Bristol, its Cathe-

dral, its street improvements: he even inserts hints to the pro- 690
jectors of these last, in a local paper: nay, he will forestall his
mother's intended visit to him at London, and return to Bristol by Christmas: and when somebody suggested, just before
his departure, that his professed hatred for the city was connected with ill-treatment received there, he returns, indig- 695
nantly, "He who without a more sufficient reason than *commonplace scurrility* can look with disgust on his native place,
is a villain, and a villain not fit to live. I am obliged to you for
supposing *me* such a villain!" Why then, without this hatred
or disgust, does he leave Bristol? Whence arises the utmost 700
distress of mind in which the mad "Will," whereby he an-
nounced his intention of committing suicide, is written? On
being questioned concerning it "he acknowledged that he
wanted for nothing, and denied any distress on that account."
"The distress was occasioned," says Dr. Gregory, "by the re- 705
fusal of a gentleman whom he had complimented in his
poems, to accommodate him with a supply of money." Here
are his own reasons. "In regard to my motives for the supposed rashness, I shall observe that I keep no worse company
than myself: I never drink to excess, and have, without van- 710
ity, too much sense to be attached to the mercenary retailers of
iniquity. No: it is my PRIDE, my damned, native, unconquerable pride, that plunges me into distraction. You must know
that nineteen-twentieth of my composition is Pride. I must
either live a Slave, a Servant; to have no Will of my own, no 715
Sentiments of my own, which I may freely declare as such; or
DIE. Perplexing alternative! But it distracts me to think of
it — I will endeavour to learn Humility — but it cannot be
HERE."

That is, at Bristol. It is needless for us here to interpose 720

127

that our whole argument goes, not upon what Chatterton said, but what he did: it is part of our proof to show that all his distress arose out of the impossibility of his saying any thing to the real purpose. But is there no approximation to the truth in what has just been quoted? Had he *not* reduced himself to the 725 alternative of living, as Rowley's transcriber, "a slave, with no sentiment of his own which he might freely declare as such," or "dying?" And did not the proud man — who, when he felt somewhat later that he had failed, would not bring his poverty to accept the offer of a meal to escape "dying" — so- 730 licit and receive, while earlier there was yet the hope of succeeding, his old companions' "subscription of a guinea apiece," to enable himself to break through the "slavery?" This, then, is our solution. For this and no other motive — to break through his slavery — at any sacrifice to get back to truth — 735 he came up to London.

It will, of course, be objected, that Chatterton gave the very reasons for his desire to obtain a release from Bristol that we have rejected. But he was forced to say something, and what came more plausibly? To Walpole the cause assigned 740 was, "that he wished to cease from being dependant on his mother;" — while, by a reference to his indenture of apprenticeship, we find him to have been supplied with "meat, drink, clothing, and lodging" by his master. To others the mercantile character of Bristol is made an insuperable objection; — 745 and he straightway leaves it for Holborn. As who, to avoid the smell of hemlock, should sail to Anticyra! It may also yet be urged — as it has been too often — that Chatterton gave to the very last, occasional symptoms that the fabricating, falsifying spirit was far from extinct in him. "He would 750 turn Methodist preacher, found a new sect," &c. Now no one

128

can suppose, and we are far from asserting, that at word of
command, Chatterton wholly put aside the old habit of imposing upon people — if that is to be the phrase. But this
"imposing upon people" has not always that basest meaning. 755
It is old as the world itself, the tendency of certain spirits to
subdue each man by perceiving what will master him, by
straightway supplying it from their own resources, and so obtaining, as tokens of success, his admiration, or fear, or wonder. It has been said even that classes of men are immediately 760
ruled in no other way. Poor Chatterton's freedom from some
such tendency we do not claim. He is indeed superior to it
when alone, in the lumber-closet on Redcliff Hill, or the lath-
walled garret at Shoreditch; but in company with the Thistlethwaites and Burgums, he must often have felt a certain 765
power he had, lying dormant there, of turning their natures
to his own account. He, "knowing that a great genius can
effect any thing, endeavoured in the foregoing poems to represent an Enthusiastic Methodist, and intended to send it to
Romaine, and impose it on the infatuated world as a reality;" 770
— but Now, no sooner is the intellectual effort made than the
moral one succeeds, and destroying these poems he determined to kill himself. Every way unsuccessful, every way
discouraged, the last scene had come. When he killed himself, his room was found "strewn thick over with torn papers." 775

To the Rowley forgeries he had recurred but in one instance, the acknowledgment of which by a magazine only
appeared after his death. He had come to London to produce works of his own; writings he had hoped to get some
hearing for. "At the Walmsleys," says Sir Herbert Croft, "he 780
used frequently to say he had many writings by him, which
would produce a great deal of money, if they were printed.

To this it was once or twice observed, that they lay in a small compass, for that he had not much luggage. But he said he had them, nevertheless. When he talked of writing some- 785 thing which should procure him money to get some clothes — to paper the room in which he lodged; and to send some more things to his sister, mother, and grandmother — he was asked why he did not enable himself to do all this by means of those writings which were 'worth their weight in gold.' 790 His answer was, that 'they were not written with a design to buy old clothes, or to paper rooms; and that if the world did not behave well, it should never see a line of them.' "

It behaves indifferently, we think, in being so sure these were simply fresh books of the "Battle of Hastings," or re- 795 modellings of "the Apostate." Look back a little, and see to what drudgery he had submitted in this London, that he could but get the means at last of going on his own ground. "A History of England" — "a voluminous history of London; to appear in numbers the beginning of next week" — "neces- 800 sitates him to go to Oxford, Cambridge, Lincoln, Coventry, and every collegiate church near." — *Any thing but Rowley!* And when the hopes he had entertained of engaging in such projects fail him, he cheerfully betakes himself to the lowest of all literary labour. He writes any thing and every thing 805 for the magazines. Projects the Moderator; supports the Town and Country; "writes, for a whim, for the Gospel Magazine;" contributes to the London, Middlesex Freehold-ers', Court and City; — and Registers and Museums get all they ask from him. Thus, we say, with these ultimate views, 810 was he constantly at work in this London pilgrimage; at work, heart and soul; living on a halfpenny roll, or a penny tart, and a glass of water a day, with now and then a sheep's

tongue; writing all the while brave letters about his happi- 815
ness and success to his grandmother, mother, and sister at
Bristol, the only creatures he loved as they loved him; and
managing, in as miraculous a way as any of his old exercises
of power, to buy them china, and fans, and gowns, and so
forth, out of his (we cannot calculate how few) pence a day;
— being, as such a genius could not but be, the noblest-hearted 820
of mortals. To be sure he had better have swept a crossing in
the streets than adopted such a method of getting bread and
water; but he had tried to find another outlet till he was sick
to the soul, and in this he had been driven to he resolved to
stay. If he could, he would have got, for instance, his liveli- 825
hood as a surgeon. "Before he left Bristol, Mr. Barrett," says
his sister, "lent him many books on surgery, and I believe he
bought many more, as I remember to have packed them up to
send to him in London;" and almost the only intelligible
phrase in a mad letter of gibberish, addressed to a friend about 830
the same time, is to the effect that "he is resolved to forsake
the Parnassian mount, and would advise that friend to do so
too, and attain the mystery of composing *smegma*" — *oint-
ment* we suppose. But nobody would help him, and this way
he was helping himself, though never so little. 835

Sufficient for the Magazine price and Magazine purpose
was the piece contributed. "Maria Friendless" and the
"Hunter of Oddities" may be a medley of Johnson and
Steele; — the few shillings they brought, fully were they
worth, though only meant to give a minute's pleasure. As 840
well expect to find, at this time of day, the sheep's tongues on
which he lived unwasted, and the halfpenny loaves no way
diminished, as find his poor "Oratorio" (the price of a gown
for his sister), or bundle of words for tunes that procured

these viands, as pleasant as ever. "Great profligacy and tergi- 845
versation in his political writings!" is muttered now, and was
solemnly outspoken once, as if he were not in some sort still
a scrivener — writing out in plain text-hand the wants of all
kinds of men of all kinds of parties. Such sought utterance,
and had a right to find it — there was an end. There might be 850
plenty of falsehood in this new course, as he would soon have
found; but it seemed as truth itself, compared with the old
expedients he had escaped from. The point is, *No more
Rowley*. His connexion with the Magazines had commenced
with Rowley — they had readily inserted portions of his 855
poems — and we cannot conceive a more favourable field of
enterprise than London would have afforded, had he been
disposed to go on with the fabrication. No prying intimates,
nor familiar townsmen, in Mrs. Angel's quiet lodging! He
had the ear, too, of many booksellers. Now would have been 860
indeed the white minute for discoveries and forgeries. He
was often pressed for matter; had to solicit all his Bristol acquaintance for contributions (some of such go under his own
name now, possibly); but with the one exception we have alluded to (affecting for a passage in which his own destitute 865
condition is too expressly described to admit of mistake) —
the Ballad of Charity — *Rowley was done with*.

We shall go no farther — the little we proposed to attempt,
having here its completion — though the plastic and co-ordi-
nating spirit which distinguishes Chatterton so remarkably, 870
seems perhaps stronger than ever in these few last days of his
existence. We must not stay to speak of it. But ever in Chatterton did his acquisitions, varied and abundant as they were,
do duty so as to seem but a little out of more in reserve. If
only a foreign word clung to his memory, he was sure to re- 875

produce it as if a whole language lay close behind — setting sometimes to work with the poorest materials; like any painter a fathom below ground in the Inquisition, who in his penury of colour turns the weather-stains on his dungeon wall into effects of light and shade, or outlines of objects, and 880 makes the single sputter of red paint in his possession go far indeed! Not that we consider the mere fabrication of old poetry so difficult a matter. For what *is* poetry, whether old or new, will have its full flow in such a scheme; and any diffi- culty or uncouthness of phrase that elsewhere would stop its 885 course at once, here not only passes with it, but confers the advantage of authenticity on what, in other circumstances, it deforms: the uncouthness will be set down to our time, and whatever significancy may lurk in it will expand to an original meaning of unlimited magnitude. But there is fine, the finest 890 poetry in Chatterton. And surely, when such an Adventurer so perishes in the Desert, we do not limit his discoveries to the last authenticated spot of ground he pitched tent upon, dug intrenchments round, and wrote good tidings home from — but rather give him the benefit of the very last heap of ashes 895 we can trace him to have kindled, and call by his name the ex- treme point to which we can track his torn garments and aban- doned treasures.

Thus much has been suggested by Mr. Wilde's method with Tasso. As by balancing conflicting statements, inter- 900 preting doubtful passages, and reconciling discrepant utter- ances, he has examined whether Tasso was true or false, loved or did not love the Princess of Este, was or was not beloved by her, — so have we sought, from similar evidences, if Chat- terton was towards the end of his life hardening himself in 905 deception or striving to cast it off. Let others apply in like manner our inquiry to other great spirits partially obscured, and they will but use us — we hope more effectually — as we have used these able and interesting volumes.

NOTES

Browning's Reading for the Essay

SINCE the notes to this edition are concerned in good part with Chatterton's story as Browning found it in his originals, a general statement regarding the extent and direction of Browning's reading may be helpful at the outset. Two sources can account for all but a fraction of his materials. Of the two, it is clear that he drew more heavily upon the biography by John Dix, published in 1837,[1] which is the only possible source for a considerable amount of the factual detail of the Essay, as well as the biography nearest Browning in point of view. Browning also found much to his purpose, however, in the recently published edition of Chatterton of which his own study is ostensibly a review. C. B. Willcox, the anonymous editor of this work[2] and author of the life which prefaces it,[3] gave him his prime example of a biographer who had "foully outraged" Chatterton's reputation; but Browning read Willcox's biography and the extensive notes in his edition with care and with profit.

Browning did not, however, confine his reading wholly to Dix and Willcox. He found Sir Herbert Croft's *Love and Madness*[4] a valuable secondary source, especially for detail regarding Chatterton's life in London. In addition he looked into Jacob Bryant's elaborate argument for

[1] *The Life of Thomas Chatterton, Including His Unpublished Poems and Correspondence* (London, 1837). Referred to in the notes as "Dix." For further comment on Dix's biography, see above, pp. 26–27.

[2] *The Poetical Works of Thomas Chatterton, with Notices of His Life, History of the Rowley Controversy, a Selection of His Letters, and Notes Critical and Explanatory* (Cambridge, 1842). The two volumes are paged consecutively. Referred to in the notes as "*Chatterton's Works*, ed. Willcox."

[3] *The Life of Thomas Chatterton*, printed in the first volume of Willcox's edition listed above and paged throughout in Roman numerals. Referred to in the notes as "Willcox."

[4] London, 1780. Referred to in the notes as "Croft." The first of the four editions of 1780 will be quoted. For further comment on Croft's curious work, see above, pp. 22–24.

Rowley,[5] he made some use of Robert Southey and Joseph Cottle's edition of Chatterton,[6] and he read, or read in, Dr. George Gregory's *The Life of Thomas Chatterton*, probably as it appears in the first volume of Southey and Cottle's edition.[7]

Naturally there is much duplication of materials in the biographies of Chatterton and the appendices and notes to the editions of his works.[8] I have attempted in the course of several months of searching to go through each book, pamphlet, and article that could have helped Browning to his interpretation of Chatterton; but where earlier accounts contain nothing that he could not have obtained as well from Dix or Willcox — and this is true in all but occasional instances — I have assumed that Browning in his somewhat hurried preparation of his study stayed fairly close to his major sources. The limits of his reading cannot be stated with precision, but absolute exactness on this point seems relatively unimportant. The important question, at least for the purposes of this edition, is how far Browning's imagination took him beyond the ac-

---

[5] *Observations upon the Poems of Thomas Rowley, in Which the Authenticity of Those Poems Is Ascertained* (London, 1781). Referred to in the notes as "Bryant".

[6] *The Works of Thomas Chatterton* (London, 1780), 3 vols. Referred to in the notes as "*Chatterton's Works*", ed. Southey and Cottle."

[7] Quoted in the notes as it appears in Southey and Cottle and referred to as "Gregory". On November 23, 1845, Browning wrote Alfred Domett: "Chatterton can only go without food a certain number of hours, so he ends it, while at that moment some benevolent man (see his name in Southey, I think) is actually started on his way to Bristol 'to inquire into the circumstances of, and, if necessary, assist the author.'" — *Robert Browning and Alfred Domett*, edited by Frederic G. Kenyon (London, 1906), p. 117. Gregory (pp. lxx–lxxi) tells of Dr. Fry's tardy journey to Bristol. Whatever the source of Browning's statement in his letter to Domett, he is apparently quoting from memory; no account, to my knowledge, has anything resembling his phrasing.

[8] Browning could conceivably have been familiar, for example, with "The Life of Thomas Chatterton" by Alexander Chalmers (*The Works of the English Poets*, edited by Alexander Chalmers, London, 1810, XV, 367–379); but he probably found his single brief quotation from this work in Dix (see note 89 below). Browning could have read Horace Walpole's *A Letter to the Editor of the Miscellanies of Thomas Chatterton* as it originally came from the press at Strawberry Hill in 1779 or as it appeared in *The Gentleman's Magazine* in 1782 or as Dix reprinted it in his biography of Chatterton. Browning probably read it only in Dix, where he also had at hand other items of Walpole's correspondence from which he quotes.

Notes

counts that could have carried him farthest; and that is the question underlying the majority of the notes that follow.

Notes to the text of the Essay are numbered serially for convenience in cross-referencing. The line number following the serial number marks the beginning of the passage to be discussed.

1. Line 1. The Essay on Chatterton appeared originally in *The Foreign Quarterly Review* for July, 1842 (XXIX, 465–483). Like other articles in the *Foreign Quarterly*, it was purportedly a lengthy review rather than an independent study. No title headed the article, though a running title "Tasso and Chatterton" was used for succeeding pages. The title *Essay on Chatterton* has been adopted for this edition, since only the first seven paragraphs of the Essay have to do primarily with Tasso, and even these are pointed toward Browning's study of Chatterton.

It is probable that Browning wrote the whole of the Essay within the five weeks preceding July 1, 1842, the day on which the July *Foreign Quarterly* was published (see *The Athenaeum* for June 25, 1842, p. 572). Browning may, to be sure, have had his copy of Wilde's *Conjectures and Researches* somewhat earlier in the year. *The Edinburgh Review* for July entered Wilde's work in its "List of New Publications from April to June, 1842" (CLII, 393); in America, Wilde had been reviewed in the January, 1842, issue of at least two periodicals (*The Dial*, II, 399–407; and *The Knickerbocker*, XIX, 78–82). But it seems clear from Browning's statements in lines 113–126 of the Essay that he did not begin writing until after he had secured Willcox's edition of Chatterton. Even if he received a reviewer's copy, Browning could not well have had Willcox long before May 27, 1842. *The Spectator* places this work among "Publications Received from May 27th to June 2d" in its issue of June 4 (p. 546); *The Athenaeum's* weekly "List of New Books" includes it on May 28 (p. 477). An advertisement in *The Athenaeum* for June 4 (p. 492) announces Willcox's edition as published on that day.

2. Line 8. In lamenting the state of Italian libraries, Browning is largely echoing Wilde's *Conjectures and Researches*, I, 140–141, but the tone and stress of Browning's remarks probably owe something to his

137

own experiences. In the spring of 1838 he had visited Italy to collect materials for *Sordello*. See William Hall Griffin and Harry Christopher Minchin, *The Life of Robert Browning* (London, 1938), pp. 93–103, and DeVane, *A Browning Handbook*, pp. 75–80.

3. Line 10. "Then a lord on whose hand the king leaned answered the man of God, and said, Behold, if the Lord would make windows in heaven, might this thing be? " — II Kings 7:2.

This rarely quoted passage seems to have made an impression upon Browning's mind, for he had already alluded to it in *Sordello:*

> Meanwhile where's the hurt
> To keep the Makers-see on the alert
> At whose defection mortals stare aghast
> As though Heaven's bounteous windows were slammed fast
> Incontinent?

I quote from the first edition (London, 1840), p. 125.

4. Line 27. Browning draws upon Wilde throughout this paragraph and the two paragraphs that follow. See *Conjectures and Researches*, I, 10, 13, 180–181; II, 164, 166.

5. Line 38. "For if they do these things in a green tree, what shall be done in the dry?" — Luke 23:31.

6. Line 46. The "popular notion" that Tasso was imprisoned because of his avowals of love for Leonora d'Este, and that his madness was a mere pretence assumed at the Duke Alfonso's command, has been long discredited. See, for example, William Boulting, *Tasso and His Times* (London, 1907), pp. 98–101, 143–144.

7. Line 82. Browning remakes Wilde's method and matter to his own purposes even as he praises them. See above, pp. 80–81, where the nature of *Conjectures and Researches* and Browning's relation to this work are discussed at length.

8. Line 130. The pertinent passage from Thomas Campbell's *Specimens of the British Poets* is given in *Chatterton's Works*, ed. Willcox, p. 395n.

9. Line 137. For Wilde's commentary referred to here, see *Conjectures and Researches*, I, 11–13.

10. Line 140. In this sentence, and in the one that follows, Brown-

ing is aiming at Chatterton's biographers in general, and Willcox in particular. Willcox had employed Wordsworth's famous phrase in a passage that Browning must have found especially objectionable:

It is not our intention to profane the chamber of death, or to pourtray with unavailing and thankless minuteness, the dark imaginings and mental convulsions of "the sleepless boy that perished in his pride." The fearful retrospect and the gloomy anticipation — the bitter thoughts, inflamed and exasperated by the knowledge of what he might have been, contrasted with the consciousness of what he was . . . are to be realized by the thinking and sympathetic heart alone. (Page cxxxix.)

Elsewhere in his *Life*, Willcox had laid stress upon Chatterton's pride and his persistence in falsehood with equal positiveness:

The proud boy held on his course, "unslacked of motion," for more than a twelvemonth afterwards [from his dealings with Walpole to the time of his death], manifesting the same passion for imposing upon the credulity of others. (Page cvii.) . . . who shall say, had his pride permitted him to live, how triumphantly hereafter he would have asserted his dignity of character, when experience had taught him the value of truth, and the security of virtue? (Page lxxiii.)

But Browning would hardly have quoted Wordsworth's phrase in such a disparaging context if he had not already felt much of the antipathy toward Wordsworth which was to reach vehement expression in *The Lost Leader*, written, probably, less than a year later (see DeVane, *Handbook*, pp. 143–146).

11. Line 142. Throughout the Essay Browning employs his characteristic idiom in discussing the problem of Chatterton's morality. Compare Browning's language in this sentence, for example, with the following passages from *King Victor and King Charles*, published but four months before the Essay:

> *Charles.* It is God's province we usurp on, else.
> Here, blindfold through the maze of things we walk
> By a slight clue of false, true, right and wrong;
> All else is rambling and presumption. I
> Have sworn to keep this kingdom: there's my truth.
> *Victor.* Truth, boy, is here, within my breast;
>   and in

Your recognition of it, truth is, too;
And in the effect of all this tortuous dealing
With falsehood, used to carry out the truth,
— In its success, this falsehood turns, again,
Truth for the world.   (II.i.283–293)

[Victor is, of course, perverting the right terms to a wrong argument.]

Charles. Ah, no question! You against me too!
You'd have me eat and drink and sleep, live, die
With this lie coiled about me, choking me!   (II.ii.572–574)

12. Line 166. Chatterton's "earliest and most partial biographer" was Mrs. Newton, Chatterton's sister, who wrote a brief sketch of her brother's life for Sir Herbert Croft. Mrs. Newton's intentions were better than her spelling, which Croft nevertheless thought worth reproducing: "When in the school we were informd by the usher, his master depended on his verasity on all occations." (Croft, p. 145.)

Browning makes considerable use of Mrs. Newton's account. He probably knew it both as it is given in Croft (pp. 143–147) and as it appears with improvements in spelling and punctuation in *Chatterton's Works*, ed. Southey and Cottle (III, 459–465). Since Browning does not follow the tortured spelling of Croft's version, I quote hereafter from Southey and Cottle, though Browning may have used Croft and done his own correcting. Browning quotes loosely from Mrs. Newton's sketch as from other materials, and his punctuation offers no trustworthy clue to his exact source. Neither Dix nor Willcox printed Mrs. Newton's narrative.

13. Line 180. The first five sentences of this paragraph are remarkably close to Browning's veiled verse autobiography, *Pauline* (quoted below from the first edition, London, 1833). The hero of *Pauline* likewise had sought at first "to compete with, or prove superior to, the world's already recognised idols" through a process of imitation, until his genius also achieved "faith in itself":

I rather sought
To rival what I wondered at, than form
Creations of my own; so much was light
Lent back by others, yet much was my own.
I paused again — a change was coming on,

I was no more a boy — the past was breaking
Before the coming, and like fever worked.
I first thought on myself — and here my powers
Burst out.   (390–398)

The hero of *Pauline*, it is true, continued to feel the influence of Shelley.
But his genius refused after a time to take "the performance or method
of another for granted"; it came to supersede these "by processes of its
own":

witness this belief
In poets, tho' sad change has come there too;
No more I leave myself to follow them:
Unconsciously I measure me by them.   (691–694)

His genius was already reaching for, though it had not yet attained, the
next stage described in the Essay, in which genius sees "cause for faith
in something external and better" and sets about its true mission through
subjugation of self to a "moral end and aim":

The soul would never rule —
It would be first in all things — it would have
Its utmost pleasure filled, — but that complete
Commanding for commanding sickens it.
The last point that I can trace is, rest beneath
Some better essence than itself — in weakness;
This is "myself" — not what I think should be,
And what is that I hunger for but God?   (814–821)

Sordello follows much the same course, though his development is complicated by the special qualities of his nature. He perishes for lack of
complete submission to "Something external and better." See *Sordello*,
I, 893–901; II, 59–88, 147–169, 395–397, 492–93, 562–586; VI,
26–603.

14. Line 227. George Psalmanazar (1679?–1763), a French impostor who came to London in 1703, excited great interest for five years
by posing as a native of Formosa. He translated the Anglican catechism
into "Formosan" (a language of his own invention) and published in
1704 a "history" of Formosa which deceived many eminent men. After
detection, he lived soberly and became an accomplished scholar. He was
one of the principal authors of the *Universal History*.

Notes

Horace Walpole had linked Chatterton's name with both Psalmanazar and James Macpherson:

> Psalmanazar, the prototype of Chatterton, as you and I coincided in thinking, though he reformed his morals and died a virtuous man, which we cannot be sure would have been Chatterton's case, seemed, though always a very sensible man, to have exhausted his inventive faculties in his creation of Formosa. [*A Letter to the Editor of the Miscellanies of Thomas Chatterton*, quoted in Dix, pp. 116–117.]

> I believe Mac Pherson's success with Ossian was more the ruin of Chatterton than I. [A letter "To the Rev. Mr. [William] Cole," quoted in Dix, p. 104.]

15. Line 236. In this paragraph, Browning follows Dix, but with interesting variations:

> The new bridge at Bristol was finished some time in the month of September, 1768, and in October there appeared, in Felix Farley's Bristol Journal, the following account of the ceremonies observed at the opening of the old structure; the manuscript being accompanied by the following note to the printer. [The note and the manuscript are then quoted in entirety.]
>
> This article, as may readily be imagined, excited considerable curiosity amongst the literati of Bristol. It evinces strong inventive powers, and an uncommon knowledge of ancient customs; and is so specific, appropriate, and characteristic, that, when we remember it to be produced by a boy not yet sixteen, it must be regarded as a real wonder.
>
> The attention of Bristol was now awakened, and many of the citizens applied to Mr. Farley for a sight of the original and the name of the transcriber. Mr. F., however, only knew that it had been brought to his office by a stranger; but some time after, Chatterton presenting another piece for insertion in the same paper, suspicion attached itself to him, with regard to the authorship of the ancient manuscript. The youth was at first very unwilling to discover whence he had the original. To the threats of those who treated him (agreeably to his age and appearance) as a child, he returned nothing but haughtiness and a refusal to give any account: but what threats failed to do, milder usage and promises of patronage effected. His first account was, that he was employed to transcribe the contents of certain ancient manuscripts by a gentleman, who had also engaged him to furnish complimentary verses, inscribed to a lady with whom that gentleman was in love. This account not being deemed satisfactory, he was further questioned, and, at last, he stated that he had received the manuscript of "the Fryars passing over the Old Bridge," with many other ancient manuscripts, from his father, which he had found in an old chest in the muniment room, on the north side of Redcliff Church. (Dix, pp. 31–34.)

16. Line 239. In giving the variant *Mayor's*, Browning is taking cognizance of Willcox's text of Chatterton's note to the printer: "The original MS. in Chatterton's handwriting is preserved in the British Museum. It is there called 'The description of the MAYOR's passing over the Bridge,' and not the 'Fryars,' [*sic*] as hitherto printed." (Willcox, p. lxiv n.)

17. Line 241. Both Willcox (p. liv) and Dix (as quoted in note 15) speak of "the literati of Bristol."

18. Line 251. Here, as elsewhere, Browning quotes very loosely. He is closest to Dix (quoted in note 15).

19. Line 255. "The father of Chatterton was, in the early part of his life, a writing master to a classical school; he afterwards became sub-chaunter of the Cathedral of Bristol." (Dix, p. 2.) Browning apparently uses *parish clerk* as a synonym for *sub-chaunter*. Willcox (p. xvii) calls Chatterton's father a "writing-usher." Croft (p. 127) and *Chatterton's Works*, ed. Southey and Cottle (III, 496) make him a sexton. Dix (p. 2) rightly denies that Chatterton's father was ever a sexton.

20. Line 272. Chatterton's dealings with Henry Burgum do not sort well with Browning's interpretation of the Boy Poet. Both Willcox (pp. xl–xlvii) and Dix (pp. 17–23) make the Burgum Pedigree Chatterton's first resort to Rowley, and place it in his years at Colston's School, long before the opening of the New Bridge occasioned his writing the manuscript which Browning wishes to consider Chatterton's first false step (lines 257–259). Both Willcox and Dix treat Burgum's Pedigree as a clever hoax that demonstrates Chatterton's early powers at duping his elders. The following excerpt is from Dix (pp. 19–21):

We may conceive the exultation of Mr. Burgum, when he first perused this singular document, on finding that he was descended from Simon de Leyncte Lyze, alias Lenliz [*sic*], in the reign of William the Conqueror, who married Matilda, daughter of Waltheof, Earl of Northumberland, Northampton, and Huntingdon, of Burgham Castle, in Northumberland. Not doubting the validity of the record, in which his own honours were so deeply implicated, he presented the poor blue-coat boy, who had been so fortunate in *finding* so much, and so assiduous in his endeavours to collect the remainder, with the plebeian remuneration of *five shillings*. Five shillings, however, was perhaps more by half-a-crown than poor Chatterton had expected to receive; and observing that Mr. Burgum thought it unnecessary to question him very minutely as to the miraculous manner in which this precious document was preserved for so many ages, amid the revolution of states and the decay of empires, he, a fortnight afterwards, presented the pewterer with a second book, being a supplement to the pedigree, bearing the following title. "Continuation of the Account of the Family of the De Burghams, from the Norman Conquest to this time, by T. Chatterton."

In this second part, to flatter his Maecenas, as well as to remove suspicion, Chatterton introduced one of the identical poems which he said he had found in the muniment room, in the true old English, with a modernization by himself. But the singularity was augmented by its being found that the following *genuine* old poem, entitled, "the Romaunte of the Cnyghte" was absolutely written by John De Burgham, one of Mr. Burgum's own ancestors! who was, according to Chatterton, "the greatest ornament of his age;" and whom he introduces in the following familiar way: "To give you, (Mr. Burgum) an idea of the poetry of the age, take the following piece, wrote about 1320." [Dix then quotes the poem in its entirety.]

For the better information of Mr. Burgum, Chatterton modernized this poem, and so delighted was the pewterer with the idea of his being descended from one of the sons of Parnassus, that he presented his informant with a second five shillings. This pedigree, being, as Mr. Cottle justly states, "one of the most ingenious and complicated of Chatterton forgeries," is contained in two volumes, each the size of a school-boy's copy book, and is reprinted, at the end of this work.

21. Line 284. In this paragraph Browning gives the key to a problem that had remained unsolved since Bryant first propounded it in 1781: where did Chatterton, lacking a knowledge of Latin and Greek, find his materials for Rowley's *Sermon*, which quotes understandingly from both languages? In actuality the *Sermon*, as Browning states, is a "mere cento" of passages from John Hurrion's six sermons on *The True Divinity of the Holy Spirit Proved from Scripture*, first published in 1734. So far as I have been able to find, the Essay is unknown to students of Chatterton, and Rowley's indebtedness to Hurrion has remained a secret. The process by which Chatterton created the *Sermon* from the pages of Hurrion is presented in detail below in the Appendix.

22. Line 291. Jacob Bryant published *Observations upon a Treatise . . .* [on] *the Plain of Troy* in 1795 and *A Dissertation concerning the War of Troy* probably in 1796 (both volumes, incidentally, are quartos, and the treatise on Rowley octavo). Willcox (p. clvii) speaks of Bryant as "the intrepid denier of the existence of Troy," and Browning may

not have looked further. Bryant held that the Trojan War was a fiction, and that Phrygian Troy had never existed. For Bryant's remarks on Rowley's *Sermon*, see Appendix.

23. Line 296. Browning may have looked through Hurrion's sermons in the Edinburgh edition of 1798 (which I have been unable to consult) or in *The Whole Works of the Rev. John Hurrion* (London, 1823), III, 3–122. Cyprian's Latin, as Browning surmised, is quoted in the first edition (see Appendix).

24. Line 339. Mrs. Newton in her letter to Sir Herbert Croft had mentioned these paraphrases of her brother's:

At twelve years old, he was confirmed by the bishop: he made very sensible, serious remarks on the awfulness of the ceremony, and his own feelings and convictions during it. Soon after this, in the week he was door-keeper, he made some verses on the last day, I think about eighteen lines; paraphrased the ninth chapter of Job; and, not long after, some chapters in Isaiah. (*Chatterton's Works*, ed. Southey and Cottle, III, 460–461.)

25. Line 356. Browning's note inscribed in his copy of *Pauline* probably in 1837 (DeVane, *Handbook*, pp. 39, 45) is of interest here. Browning, also, had approached the world obliquely:

The following Poem was written in pursuance of a foolish plan which occupied me mightily for a time, and which had for its object the enabling me to assume and realize I know not how many different characters: — meanwhile the world was never to guess that "Brown, Smith, Jones and Robinson" (as the spelling books have it) the respective authors of this poem, the other novel, such an opera, such a speech, etc., etc., were no other than one and the same individual. The present abortion was the first work of the *Poet* of the batch, who would have been more legitimately *myself* than most of the others: but I surrounded him with all manner of (to my then notion) poetical accessories, and had planned quite a delightful life for him.
Only this crab remains of the shapely Tree of Life in this Fool's paradise of mine. — R.B. (Griffin and Minchin, *Life*, 1938, pp. 56–57.)

26. Line 364. Browning quotes loosely from Chatterton's "manuscript" concerning the opening of the Old Bridge, possibly from Dix, p. 32.

27. Line 369. Browning's quotation is from Chatterton's second letter to Dodsley, given in full below in note 37.

28. Line 384. In the lengthy sentence that follows, Browning is drawing upon the testimony of Chatterton's friends John Rudhall and Edward Gardner:

> Mr. Rudhall . . . states, with reference to the parchment on which the bridge account was written, that "when Chatterton had written on the parchment, he held it over the candle, to give it the appearance of antiquity, which changed the colour of the ink, and made the parchment appear black and a little contracted;" and also . . . Mr. Gardner, . . . in his Miscellanies, published in 1798, writes, "once I saw him (Chatterton) rub a parchment with ochre, and afterwards rub it on the ground, saying, "that was the way to antiquate it." And again, in a letter dated October 8, 1802, "I can add but little to what I have said in the foregoing extract; Chatterton first rubbed the piece of parchment, in several places, in streaks with the yellow ochre, (the scene was a breeches maker's shop, in Maryport Street, once my father's wine cellar, the next door towards Peter Street to Tanner's, the barber, and three doors above the Swan Inn,) then rubbed it on the ground, which was dirty, several times, and afterwards crumpled it in his hand. He said, at the conclusion of the operation, that it would do pretty well, but he could do it better were he at home. I mention the breeches maker's shop, to account for the parchment and ochre being so ready at hand. It seemed the sudden start of a moment, done without consideration; probably had he reflected, he would have perceived that it might contribute to the detection of his forgeries." (Dix, pp. 48–50.)

Being at that time extremely young, I could be but a slender judge of the extent of his literary acquirements, or of any transactions which may tend to throw light on the Rowleian controversy; yet I distinctly remember two circumstances, which strongly operate against the claim of the Bristol priest.

I saw him once rub a piece of parchment with ochre, and afterwards rub it on the ground, at the same time saying, that was the way to antiquate it, (I remember the very word,) or to give it the appearance of antiquity.

I heard him once affirm, that it was very easy for a person who had studied antiquities, and with the aid of books which he could name, to copy the style of our elder poets so exactly, that the most skilful observer should not be able to detect him — no, said he, not Mr. Walpole himself. (Gardner's *Miscellanies*, quoted in Dix, pp. 48–49n.)

29. Line 403. Browning here makes use of Mrs. Newton's letter of October 17, 1802, to Southey or Cottle:

You desire me to inform you all I know concerning Rowley's Poems; the whole of my knowledge amounts to no more than this. My Brother read to me the Poem on our Ladies Church; after he had read it several times, I insisted upon it he had made it. He begged to know what reason I had to think so; I added, his stile was easily discovered in that poem. He replied, I confess I made this, but don't you say any thing about it. When he read the Death of Sir Charles Bawdin to my Mother, she admired it, and asked him if he made it. He reply'd, I found the argument, and versified it. I never saw any parchment in my Brother's possession but the account of Canning, with several scraps of the Tragedy of Elle, on paper, of his writing, that he read to his family, as a specimen of the treasure he had discovered in the parchments; and he always spoke of the poems to his friends, as treasures he had discovered in the parchments. (*Chatterton's Works*, ed. Southey and Cottle, III, 524–525.)

30. Line 415. For the next six sentences, Browning could have obtained his materials in the form in which he quotes them only from Bryant, pp. 526, 532, 534. Browning quotes with unusual accuracy, though the italics are mainly his own.

31. Line 432. Mrs. Newton in her letter to Sir Herbert Croft:

About this time the parchments belonging to my father, that were left of covering his boys' books, my brother carried to the office: He would often speak in great raptures of the undoubted success of his plan for future life. He was introduced to Mr. Barrett and Mr. Catcott; his ambition increased daily. His spirits were rather uneven, sometimes so gloom'd, that for many days together he would say but very little, and that by constraint. At other times exceeding chearful. When in spirits, he would enjoy his rising fame; confident of advancement, he would promise my mother and me should be partakers of his success. (*Chatterton's Works*, ed. Southey and Cottle, III, 462.)

32. Line 437. Croft, p. 139.

33. Line 447. Browning apparently quotes from memory. See note 31; Croft's text of the letter (p. 145) would not have helped him to his changes.

34. Line 455. Willcox, p. cii, and *Chatterton's Works*, ed. Willcox, p. 140n, could have supplied Browning with the materials quoted in this paragraph. But Browning should have remembered the first part of

the sentence which he adapts from Chatterton's letter to Walpole, and Willcox's quotation directly beneath it:

"The stanza, if I mistake not, was used by Ischam, Gower, Ladgate, in the sense as by Rowley, and the modern gloomy seems but a refinement of the old word. Glomming, in Anglo-Saxon, is ye twilight. . ."
"As Joseph Iscam," remarks Sir Walter Scott, "is equally a person of dubious existence with Rowley, this is a curious instance of placing the elephant upon the tortoise."

35. Line 485. Stanza XLII of the *Bristowe Tragedie; or, the Dethe of Syr Charles Bawdin*:

> And none can saye butt alle mye lyfe
> I have hys [his father's] wordyes kept;
> And summ'd the actyonns of the daie
> Eche nyghte before I slept.

Chatterton's Works, ed. Willcox (p. 9), supplies in a note Thomas Campbell's citation of the last two lines, along with two other passages from the poem, as a "simple and high conception of a great and just character."

36. Line 494. Mrs. Newton's letter to Sir Herbert Croft:

A few months before he left Bristol, he wrote letters to several booksellers in London, I believe to learn if there was any probability of his getting an employment there, but that I cannot affirm, as the subject was a secret at home. He wrote one letter to Sir Horace Warpool, and, except his correspondence with Miss Rumsey, the girl I before mentioned, I know of no other. (*Chatterton's Works*, ed. Southey and Cottle, III, 463–464.)

37. Line 497. On December 21, 1768, Chatterton wrote Dodsley offering "copies of several ancient poems; and an interlude, perhaps the oldest dramatic piece extant." (Willcox, p. lxxxiii.) It is not known whether Dodsley replied. On February 15, 1769, Chatterton sent him the following curious letter:

Sir,
Having intelligence that the tragedy of Aella was in being, after a long and laborious search, I was so happy as to attain a sight of it. Struck with the beauties of it, I endeavoured to obtain a copy of it to send to you; but the present possessor absolutely denies to give me one unless I give him a guinea for a consideration. As I am unable to procure such a sum, I made search for another copy, but unsuccessfully. Unwilling such a beauteous

piece should be lost, I have made bold to apply to you: several gentlemen
of learning, who have seen it, join with me in praising it. I am far from
having any mercenary views for myself in this affair, and, was I able, would
print it at my own risque. It is a perfect tragedy; the plot clear, the language spirited, and the songs (interspersed in it) are flowing, poetical, and
elegantly simple; the similies judiciously applied, and, though wrote in the
reign of Henry the VIth, not inferior to many of the present age. If I can
procure a copy, with or without the gratification, it shall be immediately
sent to you. The motive that actuates me to do this is, to convince the
world that the monks (of whom some have so despicable an opinion) were
not such blockheads as generally thought, and that good poetry might be
wrote in the dark days of superstition, as well as in these more enlightened
ages. An immediate answer will oblige. I shall not receive your favour as
for myself, but as your agent. — I am, sir, your most obedient servant,

THOMAS CHATTERTON.

P.S. — My reason for concealing my name was, lest my master (who is
now out of town) should see my letters, and think I neglected his business.
Direct for me on Redcliffe Hill.

[An extract from *Aella* is given at this point, followed by a second post-
script:]

The whole contains about one thousand lines. If it should not suit you,
I should be obliged to you if you would calculate the expenses of printing
it, as I will endeavour to publish it by subscription on my own account.
(Willcox, pp. lxxxiii-lxxxiv.)

"There was not so much shrewdness in this manoeuvre of Chatterton's
to obtain a guinea," Willcox (p. lxxxv) remarks, "as might have been
expected from him."

38. Line 501. Browning devotes a considerable part of the Essay
to Chatterton's experiment upon Walpole. Understandably, for Chatterton's motives in the affair are crucial to Browning's argument (see lines
505–508 and lines 542–546 of the Essay). In shaping his romantic
account of the Walpole episode, Browning drew heavily on Dix, who
alone among biographers took the easy way to eloquence afforded by a
wealthy lord's refusal of patronage to an apprentice genius. Even Croft
(p. 135) had held Walpole "by no means blameable for the life or the
death of Chatterton" and had noted significantly (p. 212) that Chatterton fixed "upon the same person (Mr. W.) to introduce Rowley to the
world, whom Macpherson chose for Ossian." Willcox, though he condemned Walpole's somewhat disingenuous apologies after Chatterton's

death, could not think Walpole "was to blame" (p. xcix). Indeed, he comments upon Chatterton's proposal that Walpole write a "History of the Antiquity of the Violin" using Rowley's data:

> The note on the antiquity of the violin is curious enough, and affords another exemplification of Chatterton's ruling passion for falsifying history. There can be no doubt, had Horace Walpole offered to undertake such a work, that Rowley's pretended manuscripts would have been forthcoming, and that Chatterton would have suffered them to be printed without throwing off the mask, or confessing the imposition; supposing, all this time, that Walpole had allowed himself to have been deceived by them.

> But already, in the second letter only, here were *four* poets, of whom the world had never heard, rescued from oblivion by Thomas Chatterton. . . He must have formed a liberal opinion of the measure of Horace Walpole's credulity, which perhaps was sufficiently ample, in the success of his former experiment, to warrant any test he might think fit to administer in a second. (Pages xciv–xcv.)

Dix alone could carry Browning far toward painting a guileless and dignified Chatterton and a hypocritical Walpole; and Browning went leagues beyond even this uncritical biographer in maintaining that "there is no new 'falsehood' discernible" in the experiment upon Walpole. Compare lines 501–640 of the Essay with the following narrative from Dix:

> The conduct of Horace Walpole towards Chatterton has been the subject of various discussions; and, after the lapse of so many years, it may, by some, be thought illiberal to renew the subject; but its importance demands for it a place here, especially as Dr. Gregory, in his memoirs of the poet, has attempted to defend the conduct of the aristocrat of Strawberry Hill.

> Mr. Walpole was, at this time, engaged in some antiquarian researches; and Chatterton, who was acquainted with his "Anecdotes of Painting," forwarded him the following letter and manuscript.

LETTER I.

"Sir,

"Being versed a little in antiquities, I have met with several curious manuscripts, among which the following may be of service to you, in any future edition of your truly entertaining Anecdotes of Painting. In correcting the mistakes (if any) in the notes, you will greatly oblige,

"Your most humble Servant,
"Thomas Chatterton.

"Bristol, March 25th, Corn Street."

Notes

[Dix then quotes the whole of Chatterton's enclosure, "The Ryse of Peyncteyne in Englande, wroten by T. Rowlie, 1469, for Mastre Canynge."]

To this letter Chatterton received the following reply: —

"Arlington Street, April 21, 1769.
"Sir,

"I cannot but think myself singularly obliged, by a gentleman with whom I have not the pleasure of being acquainted, when I read your very curious and kind letter, which I have this minute received. I give you a thousand thanks for it, and for the very obliging offer you make me of communicating your manuscript to me. What you have already sent me is valuable, and full of information; but, instead of correcting you, Sir, you are far more able to correct me. I have not the happiness of understanding the Saxon language, and without your learned notes, should not have been able to comprehend Rowley's text.

"As a second edition of my Anecdotes was published last year, I must not flatter myself that a third will be wanted soon, but I shall be happy to lay up any notices you will be so good as to extract for me, and send me at your leisure; for as it is uncertain when I may use them, I would by no means borrow and detain your MSS.

"Give me leave to ask you, where Rowley's poems are to be found. I should not be sorry to print them, or at least a specimen of them, if they have never been printed.

"The abbot John's verses, that you have given me, are wonderful for their harmony and spirit; though there are some words I do not understand. You do not point out exactly the time when he lived, which I wish to know; as I suppose it was long before John al Ectry's discovery of oil painting: if so, it confirms what I have guessed, and have hinted in my Anecdotes, that oil painting was known here much earlier than that discovery or revival.

"I will not trouble you with more questions now, Sir, but flatter myself, from the urbanity and politeness you have already shewn me, that you will give me leave to consult you. I hope, too, you will forgive the simplicity of my direction, as you have favoured me with none other.

"I am, Sir, your much obliged
"and obedient humble Servant,
"Horace Walpole.
"P.S. Be so good as to direct to Mr. Walpole, Arlington Street."

In consequence of Mr. Walpole's intimation, Chatterton, on receipt of his letter, forwarded a second communication to that gentleman. It appears, from an examination of the original document, that he had written to Horace Walpole a longer letter than this, and the line and a half, which now seems to form the letter, was merely the conclusion to it; but for some unapparent reason, Chatterton *cut off* the former part, which consisted of about six lines. This defacement probably took place after the letter was returned from Walpole.

LETTER II.

*   *   *   *   *   *   *   *   *   *

"I offer you some further anecdotes and specimens of poetry, and am,
"Your very humble and obedient Servant,
"Thomas Chatterton.

"March 30, 1769,
"Corn Street, Bristol."

[Dix then quotes the whole of the "Historie of Peyncters yn Englande, Bie T. Rowlie" and some nineteen lines of poetry by "the Abbot John" which Chatterton also enclosed with his letter. A note which Chatterton appends to one passage of the "Historie," the note upon which Willcox's comment has already been given, is especially damaging to Browning's argument: "Nothing is so much wanted as a History of the Antiquity of the Violin, nor is any antiquary more able to do it than your-self. Such a piece would redound to the honour of England, as Rowley proves the use of the bow to be knowne to the Saxons, and even introduced by them."]

In one of Chatterton's letters to Walpole, (most probably it formed the subject of the part cut off from the second letter to Mr. W. after it was returned to its writer,) he frankly stated his circumstances; that he was only sixteen years of age, and the son of a poor widow, who supported him with great difficulty; that he was apprenticed to an attorney, but had a taste for more elegant studies; and expressed a wish that Mr. Walpole would assist him with his interest in emerging out of so dull a profession, by procuring him some place in which he could pursue his natural bent. He affirmed that great treasures of ancient poetry had been discovered in his native city, and were in the hands of a person who had lent him those he had transcribed. With this letter he sent some other poems, amongst which was, (says Mr. W.) an absolutely modern pastoral [*Eleanoure and Juga*], thinly sprinkled with old words.

On the receipt of this letter, Mr. Walpole wrote to a relative at Bath, to inquire into the situation and character of Chatterton: the answer was corroborative of Chatterton's description of his situation. In the meantime he had communicated the specimens of the poems he had received, to Mr. Gray and Mr. Mason, "who at once pronounced them forgeries, and declared there was no symptom in them of their being the productions of near so distant an age; the language and metres being totally unlike anything ancient."

Now came the change: the man, or rather, Horace Walpole, for that is his *proper* name, who had expressed himself as *"singularly obliged;"* who gave a thousand thanks for the "curious letter;" who stated its contents as "very valuable and full of information;" who declared, that instead of correcting the writer of that letter, he, the writer, was "far more able to correct him;" and who complimented poor Chatterton on his "learned notes;" and spoke of the Abbot John's verses as being "wonderful for their harmony and spirit:" this Horace Walpole, (when his correspondent, with hopes engendered in his breast, by the more than favourable reception of his letters, opened his circumstances to him, never doubting but that he should find a generous patron,) returned the poor author but cold approbation of his compositions; being unable, according to his own account, to help admiring the spirit of poetry which animated them. Walpole, of all men alive, had the least reason to be offended at the literary imposition attempted to be practised upon him.

> "Who wrote Otranto?"

Exclaimed the poor bard, in the bitterness of his disappointment. But Mr. Walpole, who had himself attempted to deceive the world, could not bear that one so humble as Chatterton should deceive *him*. Mac Pherson's Ossian, too, was fresh in his memory. Before he behaved so harshly to Chatterton, Mr. Walpole would have done well to have reperused his own preface to the first edition of "The Castle of Otranto," the production of his *riper* years, in which he solemnly asserts that it was found in the "library of an ancient catholic family in the north of England, and was printed at Naples, in the black letter, in the year 1529." In the second edition, the honourable author "flatters himself he shall appear *excusable* for having offered his work to the world under the borrowed personage of a translator." Thus after giving, by his "respectable example," a sanction to literary deception, he unblushingly and heartlessly asserts, in his "Vindication," that "all of the house of forgery are relations; and that, though it be just to Chatterton's memory to say his poverty never made him claim kindred with the richest or more enriching branches, yet that his ingenuity in counterfeiting styles, and, I believe, hands, might easily have led him to those more facile imitations of prose, promissory notes." "Oh! ye, (wrote the late lamented Samuel Taylor Coleridge, in reference to this remark) Oh! ye who honour the name of *man*, rejoice that this Walpole is called *a lord*."

[Dix then quotes at some length from the indignant comments upon Walpole's conduct contained in Joseph Cottle's "Essay on Rowley's Original MSS" and Edward Rushton's poem *Neglected Genius*.]

Chatterton constantly affirmed to Mr. Catcott that Horace Walpole *despised* him, from the time he made known to him his indigent circumstances, and this assertion appears to be founded on truth and justice. From the moment this intelligence reached him, the admiration, once so ardent, suddenly ceased, and that, on an occasion when new admiration ought to have been excited, and respect unspeakably augmented; instead of which he insulted the high-minded bard of Bristol, by forwarding, instead of his former deferential epistles, as cold, phlegmatic a letter of common-place advice, (considering the occasion,) as ever issued from hard-hearted dulness; and in the very act of writing it, he himself commits a forgery on the bank of morality, where he never possessed any real capital. To return, however, to the correspondence; Mr. Walpole states, that, in answer to Chatterton's letter, which contained the application for assistance in a literary way, he wrote him a kind letter, with as much kindness and tenderness as if he had been his guardian; he undeceived him about his being a person of any interest, and urged to him, that in duty and gratitude to his mother, who had straitened herself to breed him up to a profession, he ought to *labour* in it, that in her old years he might absolve his filial debt; and told him that when he *had made a fortune* he might unbend himself with the studies more consonant with his inclinations. He also told him that he had communicated his transcripts to much better judges, and that they were by no means satisfied with the authenticity of his supposed MSS. He mentioned also their reasons for concluding that the poems could not be the production of the age to which they were assigned.

The absolute certainty that Chatterton was the author of these poems, and that they were not written in the fifteenth century, should have impelled instead of prevented Mr. Walpole from assisting him. But it is a well-known fact that Horace Walpole was all his life the enemy of his brother authors; he was unjust to the dead, injurious to the living. He says he wrote him a letter of *advice*, the constant substitute with frozen souls for good offices, when they are requested: with this *"guardian"*-like letter this affectionate and Christian guardian, sent his poor ward no substantial mark of his compassion. No, with a shameful insincerity, he assumed a sympathy he did not feel; for not long afterwards, in reference to the unfortunate subject of this memoir, he made the heartless remark, *"that singing birds should not be too well fed."*

It is to be regretted that this letter is not in existence, as the only account we have of it is from the pen of Mr. Walpole himself, an authority certainly not to be implicitly relied on.

To this letter, actuated by mingled feelings of pride and mortification, Chatterton, in about a week subsequently to the writing his second letter to Mr. Walpole, replied as follows:

LETTER III.

"Sir,

"I am not able to dispute with a person of your literary character. I have transcribed Rowley's poems, &c. &c. from a transcript in the possession of a gentleman who is assured of their authenticity. St. Austin's minster was in Bristol. In speaking of painters in Bristol, I mean glass stainers. The MSS. have long been in the hands of the present possessor, which is all I know of them. Though I am but sixteen years of age, I have lived long enough to see that poverty attends literature. I am obliged to you, Sir, for your advice, and will go a little beyond it, by destroying all my useless lumber of literature, and never using my pen again but in the law.

"I am,

"Your most humble Servant,
"Thomas Chatterton.

"Bristol, April 8, 1769."

On the 14th of April, Chatterton again wrote:

LETTER IV.

"Sir,

"Being fully convinced of the papers of Rowley being genuine, I should be obliged to you to return me the copy I sent you, having no other. Mr. Barrett, an able antiquary, who is now writing the History of Bristol, has desired it of me; and I should be sorry to deprive him, or the world indeed, of a valuable curiosity, which I know to be an authentic piece of antiquity.

"Your very humble Servant,
"Thomas Chatterton.

"Bristol, Corn Street,
  "April 14, 1769.
  "P.S. If you wish to publish them yourself, they are at your service."

The letter, No. III. Mr. Walpole describes as *"rather a peevish answer,"* but the truth of his assertion is by no means proved. Chatterton said "he would not contend with a person of Mr. Walpole's learning, and desired, in his next letter, that his manuscript may be returned["] ; and had it been *very* peevish, would any one be surprised that Chatterton, thus tantalized and trifled with, should return *such* an answer to the insults he received, instead of that encouragement which he expected?

Two other letters were addressed by Chatterton to Horace Walpole, dated also on the 14th of April, 1769. He seems to have hesitated concerning the one sent on that day, as the following (the originals of which are in the British museum) were written on the same occasion, but were never forwarded.

LETTER V.

"For Horace Walpole, Esq. Arlington Street, London.
"Sir,

"As I am *now* fully convinced that Rowley's papers are genuine, should be obliged to you if you'd send copies of them to the Town and Country

Magazine, or return them to me for that purpose; as it would be the greatest injustice to deprive the world of so valuable a curiosity.

"I have seen the original from which the extracts first sent you were copied. The harmony is not so extraordinary, as Joseph Iscam is altogether as harmonious.

"The stanza Rowley writes in, instead of being introduced by Spenser, was in use 300 years before

*   *   *   *   *   *   *   *   *

by Rowley; although I have seen some poetry of that age exceeding alliterations without rhyme.

"I shall not defend Rowley's pastoral; its merit can stand its own defence.

"Rowley was employed by Canynge, to go to the principal monasteries in the kingdom to collect drawings, paintings, and all the MSS. relating to architecture: is it then so very extraordinary he should meet with the few remains of Saxon learning? 'Tis allowed by every historian of credit, that the Normans destroyed all the Saxon MSS. paintings, &c. that fell in their way; endeavouring to suppress the very language. The want of knowing what they were, is all the foundation you can have for styling them a barbarous nation.

"If you are not satisfied with these conspicuous

*   *   *   *   *   *   *   *   *

the honour to be of my opinion.

> "I am, Sir,
> "Your very humble and obedient Servant,
> "T. Chatterton.

"Bristol, Corn Street,
  "April 14, 1769."

LETTER VI.

To the same.

"Sir,

"Being fully convinced of the papers of Rowley being genuine, I should be obliged to you to return the copy I sent you, having no other. Mr. Barrett, who is now writing the History and Antiquities of the City of Bristol, has desired it of me; and I should be very sorry to deprive him, or the world, indeed, of a valuable curiosity, which I know to be an authentic piece of antiquity. However barbarous the Saxons may be called by our modern virtuosos, it is certain we are indebted to Alfred and other Saxon kings for the wisest of our laws, and, in part, for the British constitution. The Normans, indeed, destroyed the MSS. paintings, &c. of the Saxons that fell in their way; but some might be, and certainly were, recovered out of the monasteries, &c. in which they were preserved. Mr. Vertue could know nothing of the matter — 'twas quite out of his walk. I thought Rowley's

Pastoral had a degree of merit that would be its own defence. Abbot John's verses were translated by Rowley out of the *Greek*, and there might be poetry of his age something more than mere alliterations, as he was so great a scholar. The stanza, if I mistake not, was used by Ischan, Gower, Ladgate, in the sense as by Rowley, and the modern gloomy seems but a refinement of the old word. Glomming, in Anglo-Saxon, is ye twilight.

"From, Sir,

"Your humble Servant,
"T. Chatterton.

"April 14th."

When Mr. Walpole received the letters, (Nos. 3 and 4,) from Chatterton, demanding his manuscripts, he was preparing for a journey to Paris, and he either forgot Chatterton's request, or had delayed having them copied; he therefore deferred complying with the request of the writer of the letters, and proceeded on his journey, without deigning to answer his correspondent. "I *protest*," says Horace Walpole, "I do not remember which was the case; *and yet, though in a case of so little importance*, I would not utter a syllable of which I am not positively certain; nor will charge my memory with a tittle beyond what it retains." The case to Walpole *was of very little importance*, for to Paris he went, where he remained six weeks; and on his return, found the following letter on his table, which was termed singularly impertinent by the frivolous Walpole, but which has been also, by abler judges, designated as "dignified and spirited."

LETTER VII.

"Sir,

"I cannot reconcile your behaviour with the notions I once entertained of you. I think myself injured, Sir; and did you not know my circumstances, you would not dare to treat me thus. I have sent twice for a copy of the manuscripts: — no answer from you. An explanation or excuse for your silence would oblige

"Thomas Chatterton.

"July 24th."

This is the "*singularly impertinent*" letter. . . .

Mr. Walpole says, "*My heart* did not accuse me of insolence to him. I wrote an answer expostulating with him on his injustice, and renewing *good advice*; but upon second thoughts, reflecting that so wrong-headed a young man, of whom I knew nothing, and whom I had never seen, might be absurd enough to print my letter, I flung it into the fire; and wrapping up both his poems and letters, without taking a copy of either, for which I am now sorry, I returned all to him, and thought no more of him till a year and a half after." Mr. Walpole regretted that he did not take a copy of the poems sent him; it was his intention, but it was omitted, either from neglect or hurry. Surely this is an unparalleled acknowledgment of a mind boasting the desire of committing a breach of faith. One is really at a loss which to admire most, the premeditated intent of doing a mean action, or the cool indifference with which he relates what should tend to his shame and confusion.

The letters and manuscripts were returned to Chatterton in a *blank cover*, on the 4th August, 1769. Chatterton never forgave the insult he received from Walpole. Young and ardent as he was, and unaccustomed to have to do with the cold realities of life, the repulse must have been bitter indeed. (Dix, pp. 71–101.)

39. Line 527. Walpole's *A Letter to the Editor of the Miscellanies of Thomas Chatterton*:

Will any man charge me with positive insolence towards Chatterton? Did he accuse me of it in his most "acrimonious" moments? Did he impute to me any thing but distrust of his MSS.? To myself, he did impute arrogance — but on what grounds? — on my not having returned his papers on his first summons. The world must decide on the weight of that crime. I confess the charge: I tell it myself. To judge me fairly, every man must place himself in my situation. (Dix, pp. 129–130.)

40. Line 530. These verses were published for the first time in Dix (p. 102). Browning has omitted five lines which considerably lower the tone of the poem:

> Scorn I'll repay with scorn — and pride with pride; —
> Still, Walpole, still thy prosy chapters write,
> And twaddling letters to some fair indite;
> Laud *all* above thee, fawn and cringe to those
> Who for thy fame were better friends than foes;
> Still spurn the incautious fool who dares —
> *   *   *   *   *   *   *   *   *   *
> Had I the gifts of wealth and luxury shared, . . .

The asterisks mark a blank in the manuscript. On other occasions Chatterton satirized Walpole with less show of moral indignation. There appears, for example, in his curious "criticisms on an exhibition of sign paintings" concocted for the *Middlesex Journal* of May 26, 1770:

12. *A Piece of Modern Antiquity, by Horace Walpole*. This is no other than a striking portrait of the facetious Mrs. Clive. Horace, finding it too

large to be introduced in his next edition of Virtû, has returned it on the town. (Dix, pp. 218–219.)

41. Line 574. Walpole's letter to William Cole, December 30, 1781:

In the parts I did read, Mr. Bryant, as I expected, reasons admirably, and staggered me; but when I took up the poems called Rowley's, again, I protest I cannot see the smallest air of any antiquity but the old words, the whole texture is conceived on ideas of the present century. (Dix, p. 106.)

42. Line 578. Michael Tyson to William Cole, February 4, 1779:

I find, from Mason, that Mr. Walpole is about to print an account of his transactions with Chatterton; Gray and Mason both saw the poems at Mr. Walpole's house, and both pronounced them to be modern forgeries, and recommended the returning them without any further notice. (Dix, p. 105.)

43. Line 589. "Were I in England now . . . any strange beast there makes a man: when they will not give a doit to relieve a lame beggar, they will lay out ten to see a dead Indian." (*The Tempest*, II.ii.28–32.)

44. Line 590. *A Catalogue of the Classic Contents of Strawberry Hill, Collected by Horace Walpole* (London, [1842], p. 175) lists for sale on May 13, 1842:

73 A MOST INTERESTING AND VALUABLE RELIC, the red hat of Cardinal Wolsey, found in the Great Wardrobe, by Bishop Burnet, when Clerk of the Closet; from his son the Judge, it came to the Countess Dowager of Albemarle, who presented it to Horace Walpole[.] This singular and unquestionable relic is enclosed in a glass case, it will no doubt be highly prized by the collector, from its having been worn by one of the most remarkable men of England's history.

The sale of the Strawberry Hill collections, which began on April 25 and lasted for twenty-three days, attracted widespread interest. A writer in *The Athenaeum* for April 23, 1842 (p. 364) remarked that already one of the items, Benevenuto Cellini's "Silver Bell," had "made more noise in London of late than St. Paul's." Charles Kean, the actor, bid in Cardinal Wolsey's hat for £21 (Austin Dobson, *Horace Walpole: A Memoir*, London, 1893, p. 223n).

Surely the evidence which George Henry Robins, compiler of the *Catalogue* and auctioneer of the sale, adduces for the authenticity of this "unquestionable relic" leaves room for honest doubt. *Punch* (April 16, 1842, p. 196) was skeptical:

STRAWBERRY HILL — THE CARDINAL'S HAT.

Mr. George Robins is pleased to say that this *hat* was "*lying dormant*" for eight reigns, from Henry VIII. to James II. If so, it has to boast of a prodigious *long* NAP; but we still think it will not be found worth much after having been exposed to so many REIGNS!

45. Line 592. Browning, who is surely quoting from memory, manages to telescope three widely separated sentences from Walpole's *Letter*. See Dix, pp. 132, 135, 119 respectively: ". . . nor had he quitted his master, nor was necessitous, nor otherwise poorer than attorney's clerks are. . ." ". . . and hinted a wish that I would assist him with my interest in emerging out of so dull a profession, by procuring him some place, in which he could pursue his natural bent." ". . . acquaints me that he is clerk to an attorney, but, having more inclination to poetry, wishes that I would procure him a place that would enable him to follow his propensity."

46. Line 597. In speaking of "two points," Browning possibly had in mind Walpole's doubts as to the date which Chatterton had assigned to his manuscripts and Walpole's uncertainty as to whether he had received Chatterton's last letter before setting out for Paris. See Walpole's *Letter*, Dix, pp. 133, 138.

47. Line 602. Walpole's *Letter*:

He could appear to me in no light, but in that of a bold young man, who for his interest wanted to impose upon me; and who did not commence his intercourse with me in a manner to dazzle my judgment, or give me a high opinion of his own — I allude to the article in his list of great painters at Bristol. (Dix, p. 121.)

Here I must pause, to mention my own reflections. At first I concluded that somebody having met with my Anecdotes of Painting, had a mind to laugh at me, I thought not very ingeniously, as I was not likely to swallow a succession of great painters at Bristol. The ode, or sonnet, as I think it was called, was too pretty to be part of the plan; and, as is easy with all the other supposed poems of Rowley, it was not difficult to make it very modern by changing the old words for new; though yet more difficult than with most of them — you see, I tell you fairly the case. (Dix, p. 133.)

48. Line 607. See Walpole's reply to Chatterton's first letter, quoted in note 38.

49. Line 610. *Much Ado About Nothing*, I.i.218–220:

Claudio. If this were so, so were it uttered.
Benedick. Like the old tale, my lord: it is not so, nor 'twas not so, but, indeed, God forbid it should be so.

50. Line 612. Browning has perverted Walpole's meaning: "In short, I do not believe that there ever existed so masterly a genius, except that of Psalmanazar, who before twenty-two could create a language, that all the learned of Europe, though they suspected, could not detect." (*Letter*, Dix, p. 141.) But Browning's thrust is a clever one. Walpole praises Chatterton less ambiguously elsewhere. See Dix, pp. 108–109, 150–151.

51. Line 614. Walpole's *Letter*:

I saw he was, as he told me himself, a youth tied to a profession he did not like, and born with a taste for more ingenuous studies. Consider, Sir, what would be the condition of the world, what the satisfaction of parents, and what Peruvian mines must be possessed by the Mæcenases of the times, if every muse-struck lad who is bound to an attorney, every clerk,

—— born his father's soul to cross
And pen a stanza when he should engross,

should have nothing to do but draw a bill or a couplet on the patron of learning in vogue, and have his fetters struck off, and a post assigned to him under the government! The duties of office perhaps would not be too well executed by these secretaries of the muses; and though Apollo's kingdom would certainly come, King George's would not be too well served. (Dix, p. 121.)

52. Line 621. Walpole's *Letter*:

I have already said, that I should have been blameable to his mother and society, if I had seduced an apprentice from his master to marry him to the nine muses: and I should have encouraged a propensity to forgery, which is not the talent most wanting culture in the present age. All of the house of forgery are relations; and though it is just to Chatterton's memory to say, that his poverty never made him claim kindred with the richest, or most enriching branches, yet his ingenuity in counterfeiting styles, and, I believe, hands, might easily have led him to those more facile imitations of prose, promissory notes. Yet it does not appear to my knowledge that his honesty in that respect was ever perverted. (Dix, pp. 128–129.)

. . . nor was it a grave crime in a young bard to have forged false notes of hand that were to pass current only in the parish of Parnassus. (Dix, p. 137.)

I do not mean to use the term *forged* in a harsh sense; I speak of Chatterton's mintage, as forgeries of poems in ancient language; and I am persuaded that when you condemn me for not having encouraged the coiner, you only mean to insinuate, that, if I had assisted him, I might have saved him from the dismal abyss into which he plunged. (Dix, p. 120.)

53. Line 627. Browning quotes accurately, though the italics are his own. See John Pinkerton, *Walpoliana* (second edition; London [1804]), I, 105.

54. Line 644. Browning probably quotes from memory:

Under the tuition of his mother and sister he remained for nearly three years, during the latter part of which period he was much engaged in reading all the books he could procure. He scarcely ever drank any thing but water, and frequently when his mother had a hot meal, which it appears was an uncommon occurrence, he would refuse to take any thing but bread and water, alleging, as his reason, that "he had a work in hand, and he must not make himself more stupid than God had made him." (Dix, p. 6.)

55. Line 647. Mrs. Newton's letter to Sir Herbert Croft, *Chatterton's Works*, ed. Southey and Cottle, III, 463.

56. Line 650. Dix, p. 29. According to Mrs. Edkins, however, Chatterton had reason enough for wanting to leave Lambert's office:

Mrs. Edkins said she loved the boy like a child of her own: he had seldom much money to spend, and she gave him frequently, when with Lambert, money to buy paper. On hearing him say, with a sad countenance, (for when with him he always looked full of trouble) "that paper is all gone," explaining to her that Lambert had got at it and destroyed it, because written on, on subjects not appertaining to the office; and when he found his (Chatterton's) paper even in his drawer, he would frequently tax him, as if he ought not to have any, and, with great ill-nature in his manner, ask him where he got it? And on being answered, "very honestly," even this mild reply would only irritate Lambert, and he would instantly tear it, and throw it at him with great brutality, especially when covered with manuscript; and Mrs. Edkins thinks this conduct of his master grieved him most of anything, for he used to regret these ravages, not so much the letters written to friends, for those he said he could re-write, but his poetical compositions were for ever lost! . . .

This Lambert had ten pounds with him from Colston's school; and that which hurt Chatterton's feelings most, and made him speak of it with sighs was, that he was made to take his meals with the servants.

Lambert, he said, had little business, and of course the clerk had little to do; but that, like the dog in the manger, he would neither employ him or let him employ himself; and that when he wrote a paper about killing himself, as worn out with vexations, she has no doubt he did it to induce Lambert (whom he represented to her as afraid of his own shadow) to let him go; for he once told Mrs. Edkins and his mother, that he would run away, if he could not get his dismission, as he was continually insulting him and making his life miserable. (George Cumberland's "Appendix" in Dix, pp. 311–312.)

Willcox (pp. l–liii) also paints Lambert as a "vulgar, insolent, imperious" master, repeating most of the details given in Mrs. Edkins' account.

57. Line 661? *Chatterton's Works,* ed. Willcox, mentions both poets (see pp. 354n., 464n.).

58. Line 664. Browning takes his quotation from Dix:

The treatment he experienced from Mr. Lambert, who was incapable of appreciating the talents of his apprentice, seems to have been a source of great dissatisfaction to him. He was obliged to sleep in the same room with the foot boy, and take his meals with the servants. This degradation, to one possessing such pride as Chatterton, must have been mortifying in the highest degree. "We saw him," says his sister, "most evenings before nine, and he would, in general, stay to the limits of his time, which was ten. He was seldom two evenings together without seeing us. The time of his return to Mr. Lambert's, on Sunday evenings, was eight o'clock; and if by chance he ever staid with his mother over the time specified, he would say, with a sigh, 'well, I must go, I suppose, to be reproved now.' "

From all that can be ascertained, Chatterton had the greatest contempt both for his master and for the profession with which he was connected; yet Mr. Lambert bears honourable testimony to his conduct whilst he was in his service. (Pages 25–26.)

59. Line 677. Chatterton's letter to Stephens opens a curious view of the precocious boy in the months between his experiment upon Walpole and his departure for London. Dix (p. 24) supplied Browning with

the information that Chatterton's relative was a "leather breeches maker, of Salisbury." Dix prints the letter on pages 245–247:

Sir,

If you think vanity is the dictator of the following lines, you will not do me justice. No, sir, it is only the desire of proving myself worthy your correspondence, has induced me to write. My partial friends flatter me with giving me a little uncommon share of abilities. It is Mr. Stephens alone, whose good sense disdains flattery, whom I appeal to. It is a maxim with me that compliments of friends *is* more dangerous than railing of enemies. You may enquire, if you please, for the Town and Country Magazine, wherein all signed D. B. and Asaphides, are mine. The pieces called Saxon, are originally and totally the product of my muse; though I should think it a greater merit to be able to translate Saxon. As the said magazine is by far the best of its kind, I shall have some pieces in it every month; and if I vary from my said signature, will give you notice thereof. Having some curious anecdotes of paintings and painters, I sent them to Mr. Walpole, author of the Anecdotes of Painting, Historic Doubts, and other pieces, well known in the learned world. His answer I make bold to send you. Hence I began a literary correspondence, which ended as most such do. I differed with him in the age of a MS. He insists on his superior talents, which is no proof of that superiority. We possibly may publicly engage in one of the periodical publications; though I know not who will give the onset. Of my proceedings in this affair, I shall make bold to acquaint you. My next correspondent of note is Dodsley, whose collection of modern and antique poems are in every library. In this city my principal acquaintance are Mr. Barrett, now writing, at a vast expence, an ancient and modern History of Bristol; a task more difficult than the cleansing the Augean stable. Many have attempted, but none succeeded in it; yet will this work, when finished, please not only my fellow citizens, but all the world. Mr. Catcott, author of that excellent treatise on the Deluge, and other pieces, to enumerate which would argue a supposition that you were not acquainted with the literary world. To the studies of these gentlemen I am always admitted; and they are not below asking my advice in any matters of antiquity. I have made a very curious collection of coins and antiques. As I cannot afford to have a gordlabine to keep them in, I commonly give them to those who can. If you pick up any Roman, Saxon, English coins, or other antiques, even a sight of them would highly oblige me. When you quarter your arms in the mullet, say, Or, a Fess, Vert by the name of Chatterton. I trace your family from Fitz Stephen, son of Stephen, earl of Ammerle, in 1095, son of Od, earl of Bloys, and lord of Holderness.

> I am, your very humble Servant,
> Thomas Chatterton.

60. Line 685. See above, pp. 48–49, where this quotation is given in its context as an example of Browning's extremes in warping his facts to fit his theories.

61. Line 687. Browning obtains his information for the next seven lines from Chatterton's letters (Dix, pp. 277, 283, 285–287).

62. Line 696. In supplying a background for the sentences which he quotes here, Browning spun his cloth wholly from his own imagination. The strange letter from which they come seems to reflect one of Chatterton's quarrels with other young literati of Bristol (see Meyerstein, *Life*, p. 124):

[To Mr. Baster]

Damn the muses — I abominate them and their works — they are the nurses of poverty and insanity. Your smiling Roman heroes were accounted such, as being always ready to sacrifice their lives for the good of their country. He who, without a more sufficient reason than commonplace, scurrility, can look with disgust on his native place, is a villain and a villain not fit to live. I am obliged to you for supposing me such a villain.

I am,

Your very humble Servant,
Thomas Chatterton.

(Quoted from Dix, pp. 243–244.)

63. Line 701. The circumstances surrounding Chatterton's "mad 'Will,'" which seems to contain much more satire and bravado than distress, are related in Dix (pp. 233–243) as follows:

Unsuccessful in his attempt to procure Mr. Walpole's influence in his behalf, and his contempt for the duties of his profession daily increasing, he appears to have looked forward to suicide as the only means of breaking his thraldom. He frequently informed his kitchen associates at Mr. Lambert's that he would destroy himself, and used arguments to prove that such a course was justifiable. His temper, he remarked to his sister, was becoming sour from severe study, and he said it was his intention to form an acquaintance with a young female in the neighbourhood, in the hope that such a connection might prove a corrective to his austerity of temper. [An account of his correspondence with Miss Rumsey and a protestation of his freedom from "natural depravity" are given at this point in the narrative.]

Mr. Lambert's mother having heard her son's apprentice declare his suicidal intentions, became exceedingly alarmed. Mr. Lambert, however, considered Chatterton's threats to be merely the idle words of a discontented boy, and would not be convinced of their reality until he found, one day, a copy book on his desk, in which was written the following document, entitled, "the last Will and Testament of Thomas Chatterton." Dr. Gregory states, that he has been informed, on good authority, "that it was occasioned by the refusal of a gentleman, whom he had complimented in his poems, to accommodate him with a supply of money."

[Dix then quotes the "Will" in its entirety (pp. 234–242).]

Before the discovery of this will, Mr. Lambert found on Chatterton's writing desk a letter addressed to Mr. Clayfield, stating "his distresses, and that on Mr. Clayfield's receiving that letter, he (Chatterton) should be no more." At this letter Mr. Lambert, being alarmed, sent to Mr. Barrett, thinking he might persuade him from this meditated attempt on his life, who, sending immediately for Chatterton, questioned him closely upon the occasion in a tender and friendly manner, but forcibly urged to him the horrible crime of self-murder, however glossed over by present libertines; blaming the bad company and principles he had adopted. This betrayed him into some compunction, and by his tears he seemed to feel it; at the same time he acknowledged that he wanted for nothing, and denied any distress on that account. He next day sent the following letter.

"To Mr. Barrett.

"Sir,

"Upon recollection I don't know how Mr. Clayfield could come by his letter, as I intended to have given him a letter, but did not. In regard to my motives for the supposed rashness, I shall observe, that I keep no worse company than *myself*. I never drink to excess, and have without vanity too much sense to be attached to the mercenary retailers of iniquity. No; — it is my PRIDE, my damned, native, unconquerable PRIDE, that plunges me into distraction. You must know that nineteen-twentieths of my composition is pride. I must either live a slave, a servant, have no will of my own, no sentiments of my own which I may freely declare as such, or *die*. Perplexing alternative! — But it distracts me to think of it. I will endeavour to learn humility, but it cannot be here. What it will cost me on the trial heaven knows.

"I am,
"Your much obliged, unhappy, humble Servant,
"T. C."

64. Line 705. Gregory, p. 1 (fifty); but Browning follows Dix (p. 234) in omitting *occasionally* before *complimented*.

65. Line 708. It is now generally accepted that Chatterton, as Mrs. Edkins divined (note 56), wrote his suicide note "to induce Lambert . . . to let him go." The "Will" probably had the same purpose. Once

Lambert had discovered this second startling document upon his desk "by accident," he hurried to dismiss his apprentice. See Meyerstein, *Life*, pp. 332–347.

66. Line 714. The fact that Browning uses *twentieth* instead of *twentieths* suggests that he may have quoted from the facsimile of the letter given in Willcox opposite p. cxvi, where "19/20th" appears. In any event, putting *here* in capitals (line 719) was his own idea.

67. Line 720. Dix's narrative concerning Chatterton's departure from Bristol follows:

Discharged from the office of Mr. Lambert, and knowing but little of his profession, for in a letter written after his arrival in London, he says, referring to a clearance which Mr. Lambert demanded, "As to the clearance I am ever ready to give it; but really I understand so little of the law, that I believe Mr. Lambert must draw it out." Chatterton resolved to leave the city, where he conceived he had been treated with such indignity. The periodical press he looked forward to as an ample means of support, and he had received promises of employment from the editors of several papers and magazines. His friend, Mr. Thistlethwaite, anxious for his welfare, interrogated him as to the object of his views and expectations, and what mode of life he intended to pursue on his arrival in London. The answer he received was "a memorable one." "My first attempt," said he, "shall be in a literary way. The promises I have received are sufficient to dispel doubt; but should I, contrary to my expectations, find myself deceived, I will, in that case, turn methodist preacher. Credulity is as potent a deity as ever, and a new sect may easily be devised. But if that too shall fail me, my last and final resource is a pistol." "Most of his friends and acquaintance," according to Mr. Barrett, "contributed a guinea each towards his journey" to London, where he arrived on the 25th April, 1770; and his patron adds, "he there settled, but carried his libertine principles with him." What kind of libertinism Mr. Barrett refers to I know not: there is abundant evidence to prove that Chatterton was not the character some have represented him to have been. (Pages 249–250.)

68. Line 730. Dix, p. 290:

Mrs. Angel stated, that for two days, when he did not absent himself from his room, he went without sustenance of any kind; on one occasion, when she knew him to be in want of food, she begged he would take a little dinner with her; he was offended at the invitation, of which he hinted he was not in want, and assured her he was not hungry. Mr. Cross, also, an apothecary in Brook-street, gave evidence that he repeatedly pressed

Chatterton to dine or sup with him; and when, with great difficulty, he was one evening prevailed on to partake of a barrel of oysters, he was observed to eat most voraciously.

69. Line 741. Browning apparently forms this "quotation" from Walpole's statement in the *Letter* (Dix, p. 135): "Chatterton, in answer, informed me that he was the son of a poor widow, who supported him with great difficulty."

70. Line 742. "The indentures of his apprenticeship are now deposited in the Bristol Institution; from them it appears that Chatterton was to be found by Lambert in meat, drink, clothing, and lodging, and, by a special agreement, his mother was to wash and mend for him." (Dix, p. 25.)

71. Line 744. At least Chatterton's writings show that he was impressed by Bristol's mercantile character. In his series of criticisms upon an imaginary "exhibition of sign paintings," he includes:

11. *The genius of Bristol, by Bonner.* Represents a fish-woman sleeping on a cask: her shield a cheese, with her arms blazoned; three hogs couchant in the mire; her lance a spit, with a goose on it. There are several smaller figures in the groupe; a turn-spit dog, a sleeping alderman, and a Welch rabbit. (Dix, p. 218.)

In a letter of May 6, 1770, Chatterton writes his mother:

Bristol's mercenary walls were never destin'd to hold me — there, I was out of my element: now, I am in it — London! Good God! how superior is London to that despicable place Bristol! — Here is none of your little meannesses, none of your mercenary securities, which disgrace that miserable hamlet. (Dix, pp. 263–264.)

72. Line 747. Browning apparently has the proverb *naviget Anticyram* in mind and perhaps alludes specifically to Horace's *Satires*, ii.3.166. But the ancients sailed to Anticyras not for hemlock but for hellebore, the most popular remedy in antiquity for madness.

73. Line 751. See note 67.

74. Line 756. For echoes of this idea in Browning's poetry, see above, pp. 61–62, 74–75.

75. Line 763. It is strange that Browning should mention the "lumber-closet" as a place where Chatterton was superior to temptation, for

it was there, according to Mrs. Edkins, that he manufactured the Rowley manuscripts:

From twelve to seven, each Saturday, he was always at home, returning punctually a few minutes after the clock had struck, to get to his little room and shut himself up. In this room he always had by him a great piece of ochre in a brown pan — pounce bags full of charcoal dust, which he had from a Miss Sanger, a neighbour; also a bottle of black lead powder, which they once took to clean the stove with, and made him very angry. Every holiday almost he passed at home, and often, having been denied the key when he wanted it, (because they thought he hurt his health and made himself dirty) he would come to Mrs. Edkins and kiss her cheek, and coax her to get it for him, using the most persuasive expressions to effect his end; — so that this eagerness of his to be in this room so much alone, the apparatus, the parchments, (for he was not then indentured to Mr. Lambert) both plain as well as written on, and the begrimed figure he always presented when he came down at tea time, his face exhibiting many stains of black and yellow, — all these circumstances began to alarm them; and when she could get into his room, she would be very inquisitive, and peep about at every thing. Once he put his foot on a parchment on the floor, to prevent her from taking it up, saying, "You are too curious and clear sighted — I wish you would bide out of the room — it is my room." To this, she answered by telling him, that it was only a general lumber room, and that she wanted some parchment, some of his old Rowley's, to make thread-papers of; but he was offended, and would not permit her to touch any of them, not even those that were not written on. But at last, with a voice of entreaty, said, "Pray, don't touch any thing here," and seemed very anxious to get her away; and this increased her fears, lest he should be doing something improper, knowing his want of money, and ambition to appear like others. At last they got a strange idea, that these colours were to colour himself, and that, perhaps, he would join some gipsies, one day or other, as he seemed so discontented with his station in life, and unhappy. (George Cumberland's "Appendix" in Dix, pp. 313–314. Willcox, pp. xxxix–xli, also gives this portion of Mrs. Edkins' narrative.)

76. Line 767. For a discussion of Browning's remarkable account of Chatterton's "last scene," see above, pp. 44–47. Dix and Willcox are bald by comparison:

In the desperate circumstances in which he was now placed, his mind reverted to what he had unhappily accustomed himself to regard as a last resource. I am not of those who would defame the character of Chatterton because he committed suicide. When we remember his hopes, and the blight that fell upon them, his youth, his despair, and his extreme poverty, can the result be a matter of wonder? Insanity was hereditary in his family, and a combination of adverse circumstances acting on his too excitable mind, fostered the seeds of mental disease. "Chatterton," said Lord Byron, "*I* think was mad." The christian charity of those must be little indeed who seek to depreciate his *character* on account of the manner of his death. . .

On the 24th of August, 1770, Thomas Chatterton, at the age of seventeen years and nine months, overcome by despair and distress, terminated his clouded career by swallowing poison — according to the best authorities, *arsenic* in *water*, and died in consequence the next day. His room, when broken open, was found covered with little scraps of paper, and all his unfinished pieces were cautiously destroyed before his death. An inquest was held on his body, and he was interred in the burying-ground of Shoe-lane workhouse. (Dix, pp. 291–292.)

The hour had arrived: there was no hope, no help on earth — his prospects were blighted, and his friends had forsaken or forgotten him. . .

On the 24th of August 1770, Chatterton resolved to close his life of misery and privation. The suicide was effected by arsenic mixed in water: such at least was the opinion of the most competent authorities. On the following day his room was broken open. The floor was covered with a multitude of small fragments of paper; an evidence that he had destroyed all the unfinished productions of his marvellous intellect. There was no letter to his friends — no apologetic explanation of the terrible step which he had taken — not a single line to satisfy the curious and to console the afflicted, or to demonstrate that Chatterton had died sane or insane — Christian or unbeliever. (Willcox, pp. cxxxviii–clx.)

77. Line 775. The phrase in quotation marks seems to represent an inaccurate recalling of Dix or Willcox or Croft (see note 80).

78. Line 777. *The Town and Country Magazine* for August, 1770, issued a few days after Chatterton's death, acknowledged receipt of the *Balade of Charitie* but did not print the poem. See Croft, pp. 205–206.

79. Line 780. Croft, pp. 208–209.

80. Line 796. Dix (p. 60) mentions "the Apostate, a Tragedy" as a poem once described by Chatterton but never "brought to light." Browning, however, seems to allude especially to Croft:

His room, when it was broken open, after his death, was found, like the room he quitted at Mr. Walmsley's, covered with little scraps of paper. What a picture would he have made, with the fatal cup by his bed side, destroying plans for future *Aellas* and *Godwins*, and unfinished books of *the battle of Hastings*? (Pages 197–198.)

81. Line 798. The next five sentences reveal in miniature the eclectic process by which Browning shaped his interpretation of Chatterton from his materials. Browning's argument seems to be that Chatterton began writing "any thing and every thing for the magazines" only after he found it impossible to support himself by means of a more respectable project for writing histories. In support of his view, Browning quotes in lines 798–802 from Chatterton's letter to his sister on May 30, 1770 (Dix, pp. 275–279). This very letter, however, could have warned Browning of the perils of his argument. The next sentence after that quoted by Browning enjoins Mary to send Chatterton's "Manuscript Glossary" by means of which he manufactured Rowley. The six sentences following that describe Chatterton's plan to write political articles favoring the Lord Mayor: "But the devil of the matter is, there is no money to be got on this side of the question. Interest is on the other side. But he is a poor author, who cannot write on both sides. I believe I may be introduced (and if I am not, I'll introduce myself) to a ruling power in the Court party." A few lines farther along there appears the passage which Browning paraphrases in bolstering his contention that Chatterton had no antipathy to Bristol (lines 683–691 of the Essay). And toward the end of this same letter, after some decidedly indelicate remarks concerning a Miss Thatcher, Browning found the passage which he quotes in lines 807–808, a passage which shows that Chatterton was already contributing to the *Gospel Magazine* at the time when he described his plans for writing histories, though Browning employs it in his argument that Chatterton turned to the periodicals only after he had given up hope of supporting himself by writing histories. Browning's quotations from this letter are in each instance inexact. Probably he wrote them from memory after he had forgotten the context in which they appear.

82. Line 806. Chatterton refers in his letters to the magazines mentioned in the next four lines. See Dix, pp. 265–267, 274, 279, 283–284.

83. Line 812. "When he himself was living on a penny tart and a glass of water per day, he sent little presents to his Bristol friends, and tried, with an amiable feeling, to conceal from them his want of suc-

cess." (Dix, p. 275.) " . . . [Chatterton] lived chiefly upon a bit of bread, or a tart, and some water: but he [Chatterton's bedfellow at the Walmesleys'] once or twice a week saw him take a sheep's tongue out of his pocket . . . " (Croft, p. 192.) For Chatterton's letters describing the gifts, see Dix, pp. 282–283. Pride may have impelled Chatterton in sending these presents; he was not in dire want at the time he dispatched them (see Meyerstein, *Life*, pp. 409–412).

84. Line 823. As intimated in note 81, Browning in his contention that Chatterton tried other means of supporting himself before he resorted to writing for the periodicals has all the evidence against him. Chatterton contributed to *The Town and Country Magazine* before leaving Bristol — even as early as November, 1768. He went to London with the intention of making his living by means of the magazines and began writing for them immediately upon arriving. (See Dix, pp. 66, 250, 262.) Chatterton applied to Barrett for a recommendation as "a surgeon's mate to Africa" only after he had been four months in London, by which time it had become obvious that he could not live on what he received from editors (Dix, p. 289). Mrs. Ballance would have preferred Browning's Chatterton to her "Cousin Tommy":

> Chatterton's first residence in London was at Mrs. Walmsley's, in Shoreditch, where also lodged Mrs. Ballance, a relative of his. Mrs. Ballance describes him as having been exceedingly proud; once, when after he had been in London three weeks, she recommended him to obtain a situation in some office, he stormed about the room like a madman, and told her, that he hoped, with the blessing of God, very soon to be sent prisoner to the tower, which would make his fortune. (Dix, pp. 287–288.)

85. Line 826. "Mr. Barrett lent him many books on surgery, and I believe he bought many more, as I remember to have packed them up to send to him when in London, and no demand was ever made for them." (*Chatterton's Works*, ed. Southey and Cottle, III, 462–463.)

86. Line 830. Chatterton's "mad letter" addressed to a William Smith is a curious exercise in hard words garnered from John Kersey's *Dictionarium Anglo-Britannicum* (see Meyerstein, *Life*, pp. 430–431):

> In short, an enpynion could not contain a greater synchysis of such accidents without syzygia. I am resolved to forsake the Parnassian mount, and would advise you to do so too, and attain the mystery of composing smegma.

Think not I make a mysterismus in mentioning smegma. No; my mne-
mosque will let me see (unless I have an amblyopia) your great services . . .
(Dix, p. 245.)

The passage which Browning employs has taken on importance in recent
years. Meyerstein has identified *smegma* as a lenitive electuary for the
treatment of venereal disease. The word is used in this sense in Skelton's
Why Come Ye Not to Court. Chatterton was familiar with Skelton's
poetry. See Meyerstein's article "Chatterton's Last Days," [London]
Times Literary Supplement, June 28, 1941, p. 316.

87. Line 837. Willcox names these pieces and others like them as

light essays, modelled on those of Steele, Addison, and other writers of the
eighteenth century, but scarcely deserving of a second perusal. . . It is
quite unnecessary to comment on each of these productions: the tales apparently do not aim at originality — indeed one of them, the story of Maria
Friendless, is an old acquaintance in a new dress; it is a "masqued resurrection" of Misella in the Rambler. (Pages cxxx–cxxxi.)

88. Line 843. See Chatterton's letter to his sister, July 20, 1770
(Dix, p. 284).

89. Line 845. "[Chatterton's] deceptions, his prevarications, his
political tergiversation, &c. were such as we should have looked for in
men of an advanced age, hardened by evil associations, and soured by
disappointed pride or avarice." (Alexander Chalmers, "The Life of
Thomas Chatterton," in *The Works of the English Poets,* ed. Alexander
Chalmers, London, 1810, XV, 373.) Dix (p. 256) quotes this passage.
Both Dix and Willcox (pp. cxxvii–cxxviii) condemn Chalmers' use of
the phrase *political tergiversation,* but Browning probably detected mut-
terings of Chalmers' view in Willcox's lament that Chatterton in writing for the periodicals had

sold, Esau-like, his birthright — the vision and the faculty divine — for a
mess of pottage. How could any good come out of such a Galilee as this?
What could be looked for but that the creator should sink into the scribbler,
the poet into the buffoon — a spirit, free, uncompromising, integral, into a
character compromised, factional, and slavish? (Page cxxii.)

90. Line 854. A passage in Croft (pp. 202–203) offers an interesting contrast to the next fourteen lines of the Essay. Browning probably

had Croft's arguments in mind as he wrote, for he covers the same ground almost point for point:

After Chatterton left Bristol we see but one more of Rowley's poems, "The ballad of Charitie:" And that a very short one. What was the reason of this? Had C. given to the world all the contents of Canynge's chest? Certainly not — for he is known to have spoken of other M.S.S. both at Bristol and in town; and you have seen him write to his mother that, "had Rowley been a Londoner, instead of a Bristowyan, he could live by copying his works." Is it likely that a lad, possest of a chest full of such poems (some of which he sold for trifles to a pewterer, before he wanted money or knew its value), should, when in real distress, and when he could have lived by only copying them, part with none of them, offer not one of them to any bookseller? Ridiculous! Impossible! This was the very moment to produce them. In my own mind I am persuaded that, had C. really found the poems in an old chest, the idea of *forging* others, as like them as he could, *would now* have struck him. But, in truth, Canynge's old chest, was only his own fruitful invention. At Bristol, undisturbed by the cares, or the pleasures of the world, his genius had nothing to do but to indulge itself in creating Rowley and his works. In London, that was to be learnt which even Genius cannot teach, the knowledge of life — Extemporaneous bread was to be earned more suddenly than even Chatterton could write poems for Rowley — and, in consequence of his employments, as he tells his mother, publick places were to be visited, and mankind to be frequented. He, who fabricated such poems, in the calm and quiet of Bristol, must have been almost more than man. Had C. produced them to the world *as fast*, amidst the avocations, the allurements, the miseries of his London life, I would immediately become a convert to Rowley.

Croft implausibly suggests (pp. 206–207) that Chatterton may have committed suicide because *The Town and Country Magazine*, which rejected the *Balade of Charitie*, "doubted the existence of his friend Rowley. . . it is pretty clear that the Magazine thought C. was *the author* of Rowley's poems."

91. Line 862. Chatterton seems to offer his friends publication through his influence as a privilege conferred rather than as a favor to himself. See his letters to Thomas Cary, Henry Kator, William Smith, and others (Dix, pp. 265–267).

92. Line 865. Croft (pp. 204–205) quotes the passage and comments upon it:

Look in his glomed face, his sprite there scan,
How woebegone, how withered, sapless, dead!
Haste to thy church-glebe house, asshrewed man;
Haste to thy kiste, thy only dortoure bed!
Cold as the clay which will gre on thy head
Is charity and love among high elves;
Knightis and *Barons* live for pleasure and themselves.

This seems too plainly designed for a sketch of himself, and of the coldness with which he conceived he had been treated; especially as "the Memoirs of a Sad Dog" appeared in the Town and Country Magazines for July and August 1770: wherein C. ridicules Mr. Walpole with some humour, under the title of *Baron* of Otranto.

93. Line 873. Compare *Sordello* (London, 1840, pp. 112–113):

while from true works (to wit
Sordello's dream-performances that will
Be never more than dream) escapes there still
Some proof the singer's proper life's beneath [deeper than]
The life his song exhibits, this a sheath
To that; a passion and a knowledge far
Transcending these, majestic as they are,
Smoulder; his lay was but an episode
In the bard's life.

94. Line 877. The admiration which Browning expresses here for the ability "to work with the poorest materials" seems to be echoed in his letter to Elizabeth on August 3, 1846 (*The Letters of Robert Browning and Elizabeth Barrett Browning, 1845–1846*, London, 1898, II, 388). There he speaks of "putting, as I always have done, my whole pride, if that is the proper name, in the being able to work with the least possible materials."

95. Line 899. For comment upon this concluding paragraph of the Essay, see above, pp. 49–51, 82 ff.

APPENDIX

BROWNING AND ROWLEY'S *SERMON*

UNHISTORICAL as it is in other respects, the Essay on Chatterton does clarify biography in regard to one revealing incident in Chatterton's career, his creation of Rowley's *Sermon*. Though the *Sermon* was at one time a focal point in the Rowley Controversy, the exact means by which Chatterton, who had not enjoyed formal schooling beyond writing and accounts, managed to display a knowledge of Latin, Greek, and divinity in this work are not, I believe, known to students of Chatterton to the present day.[1]

Had the actual source of the *Sermon* been discovered in the last decades of the eighteenth century, the Rowley Controversy might have come to a more abrupt conclusion. When Rowley's words upon the "Holye Spryte" and his Latin and Greek quotations are compared to the pertinent passages in the Reverend John Hurrion's six sermons upon *The True Divinity of the Holy Spirit Proved from Scripture*,[2] the process by which Chatterton contrived to impersonate a learned ecclesiastic is revealed with a new clarity.

I

Chatterton gave the fragmentary *Sermon* to the Reverend Alexander Catcott, brother of his patron George Catcott, at some time before his departure for London. George Catcott could not persuade Chatterton

---

[1] Meyerstein (*Life*, p. 309) follows the explanation of "An Enquirer" in *The Gentleman's Magazine* for May, 1782 (given below). Bibliographies since the publication of Meyerstein's *Life* in 1930 suggest nothing new on the subject.

[2] These six sermons make up the first section of Hurrion's posthumous *The Scripture Doctrine of the Proper Divinity, Real Personality, and the External and Extraordinary Works of the Holy Spirit, Stated and Defended; in Sixteen Sermons, Preach'd at the Merchants Lecture at Pinners-Hall, In the Years 1729, 1730, 1731* (London, 1734). Browning consulted a later edition (see note 23 to the text of the Essay). I was unable to find a copy of the first edition in the United States. I wish to acknowledge the kindness of the trustees of the British Museum and the

to give or sell him the remainder of the work.[3] Later George, as an ardent Rowleyan, laid especial emphasis on this work. He lamented the omission of it from Thomas Tyrwhitt's edition of the Rowley poems in 1777 because he was sure that the piety of Rowley's remarks would have showed that Chatterton could not be the author.[4] The *Sermon* was first printed in 1778 in John Broughton's edition of the *Miscellanies in Prose and Verse of Thomas Chatterton*. In 1781, Jacob Bryant, as Browning states in the Essay (288–293), seized upon the *Sermon* as evidence of Rowley's existence, a composition clearly beyond the powers of Chatterton:

In the sermon upon the *Holy Sprite*, there is a quotation from Cyprian; and another from the Greek of Gregory Nazianzen: and in the story of John Lamington are many Latin quotations.[5] None of these were obvious, and such as a boy could attain to. Nor are they idly and ostentatiously introduced: they are all pertinent, and well adapted. In respect to the sermon upon the *Holy Sprite*, the very texture of it shews, that it was the composition of a person versed in divinity. Hence some have thought, that Chatterton accidentally lit upon an old sermon; and put it off for Rowley's. But if we allow him to have met with such an ancient composition, what inducement could he have to ascribe it to a wrong author? Consequently, can any reason be alledged, why we should not give it to the person specified? It is said, that the history of Rowley is obscure, and but lately made known. But what do we get by having recourse to a person still more in the dark; and whose history is not at all known? [6]

In April, 1782, *The Gentleman's Magazine* printed the *Sermon* with this comment:

The following Fragment has been produced as a transcript from a Sermon by Thomas Rowley, Priest, of the fifteenth century. There being little

---

officers of the Indiana University Library in affording me access to a microfilm of the work and supplying me with a larger negative of page 124, employed in making the illustration which appears below.

[3] Meyerstein, *Life*, p. 309.

[4] *Idem.*

[5] Tyrwhitt on p. 209 of his *Vindication* (discussed below) states that Chatterton could have found all the Latin quotations for the "story of John Lamington" in a common schoolroom text of *Cato's Distichs* and the *Sentences of Publius Syrus.*

[6] *Observations upon the Poems of Thomas Rowley, in Which the Authenticity of Those Poems Is Ascertained*, pp. 563–564. Rowley's Greek is quoted on p. 563n.

reason, however, to suppose that Chatterton, who apparently forged all other pieces attributed to this occult personage, could be the immediate author of such a performance, to learn from whence the ground-work of it was borrowed, is the object of the present insertion.

If any person, who has leisure and opportunity, should happen, in the course of his researches after things of greater moment, to make such a discovery, and will communicate satisfactory proof of it through the channel of this Magazine; as a small acknowledgement for his trouble, a set of books, chosen by himself, and of three guineas value, shall be at the service of the earliest satisfactory communicator. . .

The words ascribed to Cyprian are supposed not to belong to that Father. They are taken from a tract *De Cardinalibus Christi Operibus*, formerly imagined to be Cyprian's, but long since rejected by the best critics, and attributed by Bishop Fell to Arnald of Chartres, Abbot of Beauval, a contemporary and friend of St. Bernard, A. D. 1160.[7]

Next month *The Gentleman's Magazine* carried the following reply from "An Enquirer":

Wrexham, May 14.

Mr. Urban,

I will not be confident that I have discovered the *ground-work* of the fragment enquired after, p. 177; but, if your correspondent consults the latter of two sermons on the *Deity of the Son, and Holy Spirit*, by the Rev. Caleb Evans of Bristol, printed for *Buckland*, 1766, he will find the beginning very similar to the fragment; and also, upon reading the former, that Mr. *Evans's* proof of the *Deity of Christ* is agreeable to *Rowley's* reference. If too he reads p. 72 of the above sermons, Mr. *Evans* quotes *Herman Witsius*, a Dutch divine. The quotation is from his *Exercitationes in Symbolum*. Now, whether Chatterton's inquisitive genius did (as he easily might) understand so much Latin as to dip into *Witsius*, or might get it translated, it is certain that the very address to the Spirit, said to be from St. *Cyprian*, is in the beginning of *Exercit. XXIII.* and is introduced in almost the same words as in *Rowley's* fragment. I observe further, that *Witsius* has, sect. XXXII., *Rowley's* argument, "Seyncte Paulle sayeth yee are the temple of Godde," &c. and speaks of the "personne, giftes, operatyonns, &c. of the Holy Spryte;" all which Chatterton might acquire by a very shallow acquaintance with Latin, and indeed most of them by only

[7] Page 177 and note. At the end of the *Sermon*, the source of Rowley's Greek is subjoined as "Greg. Nazianz. Orat. xxx. v.I. p. 610. edit. Paris, 1639." All of this commentary and the major part of the reply of "An Enquirer" given below appear in *Chatterton's Works*, ed. Willcox, pp. 681–682n., where Browning must have read them.

reading the table prefixed to the Exercitation. I will not say where he got the curious notion, that it will be the peculiar office of the Holy Spirit to "destroye" the "worlde" (perhaps it was Mr. Chatterton's *own*), nor yet whence he had the extract from St. *Gregory*; but your correspondent will be struck with the similarity, I was going to say, *sameness*, of the supposed *Rowley's* reasoning, that "the Holy Spryte cannot bee the goode thynges and vyrtues of a man's mynde," with that of Mr. *Evans*, p. 57–60. Is not the expression, *Deity of the Spirit*, more modern than the fifteenth century? But it is in the beginning of Mr. *Evans's* Sermon.

Possibly, amongst your numerous correspondence, a more decisive reply may be given than I have; but, upon reading the fragment, it struck me as having much the air of the authors mentioned, and I could not forbear communicating my ideas. If they are not satisfactory, perhaps it may be worth while to look, if, amongst Archbishop *Leighton's Theological Lectures*, there is one on the Deity of the Spirit. I have not got the work, but the fragment is far from being unlike the style of that Divine's other works.

Yours &c.

AN ENQUIRER.[8]

Later in the same year (1782), Thomas Tyrwhitt, who had begun Rowleyan but who was no longer of the faith,[9] published his *A Vindication of the Appendix to the Poems, Called Rowley's, in Reply to the Answers of the Dean of Exeter, Jacob Bryant, Esquire, and a Third Anonymous Writer.* The *Sermon* seemed to Tyrwhitt so clearly a case in point that he engaged a Mr. Strutt to engrave a facsimile of Chatterton's quotation from the Greek of Gregory Nazianzen [10] and neatly turned Bryant's arguments against their originator in the following remarks:

I am much inclined to think myself, that the ground work of this *Fragment* was an old sermon, in which CHATTERTON found the two quotations ready to his hand. The rest, if not his own invention, was at least translated by him into the *Rowleian dialect*; as the language abounds with the same solecisms and barbarisms, which have demonstrated the spuriousness of the

[8] Pages 220–221.

[9] See L. F. Powell, "Thomas Tyrwhitt and the Rowley Poems," *The Review of English Studies*, VII (1931), 314–326.

[10] "The engraving, which is to face page 207, is finished by Mr. Strutt; and you may have it whenever you will send for it." (Tyrwhitt's letter of July 21, 1782, to his publisher, in John Nichols, *Literary Anecdotes of the Eighteenth Century*, London, 1814, VIII, 113.)

Poems. But, without having recourse to them upon this occasion, it happens, that the Greek quotation from GREGORY NAZIANZEN contains in itself the most unquestionable proof, that it was not copied from any Ms. of the XVth century. It will be allowed, I presume, that CHATTERTON could only copy the characters which he found in his original. He had not skill enough to vary the forms of the letters; to combine those which were separate, or to separate those which were connected together. We may be certain, therefore, that his transcript (involuntary errors excepted) was in all respects as like to his archetype as he could make it. But his transcript differs totally from all the specimens which I have ever seen of Greek writing in the XVth century. It appears to me to have been evidently copied from a *printed book*; but, as I do not wish to judge for others in these matters, I shall annex an exact *Fac simile* of the passage, as it stands in CHATTERTON's own hand-writing. The reader will determine, whether it could have been copied by him from any Ms. of ROWLEY.[11]

Despite the force of Tyrwhitt's *Vindication*, Rowleyans continued to push their claims, though with abating zeal, for several years, and the Bristol priest had at least one fiery adherent in 1857.[12]

2

Tyrwhitt's surmises were made with the habitual shrewdness of that eminent scholar, and it is but justice to show how clearly his facsimile points to the original of the *Sermon*. It will be noted in the illustration given opposite page 182 that Chatterton's characters are an adroit imitation of the characters which he found in Hurrion and that he divided his first line of Greek exactly as it is divided in his source. These facts, however, are secondary to the most striking detail: In Hurrion, χ in $\pi\rho o\tau\rho\acute{\epsilon}\chi\epsilon\iota$ appears directly above ϵ in $\dot{\epsilon}\pi\iota\tau\epsilon\lambda\epsilon\hat{\iota}$, and the smooth breathing above ϵ is printed very close to χ above it. Chatterton carefully inscribed this smooth breathing beneath χ, apparently mistaking it for a part of that letter; $\dot{\epsilon}\pi\iota\tau\epsilon\lambda\epsilon\hat{\iota}$, minus its smooth breathing, appears elsewhere. It is inconceivable that another printing of Gregory's lines duplicates the spacing in Hurrion and could thus lead Chatterton to make this telltale error.

But Chatterton found far more in Hurrion than the quotation from Gregory Nazianzen. Rowley's *Sermon* is in part a paraphrase of Hur-

[11] Pages 206–207. [12] See above, p. 28.

181

rion's six sermons on *The True Divinity of the Holy Spirit* and the rest seems clearly a distillation from them. It is unlikely that Chatterton made any use of the Rev. Caleb Evans' sermons as "An Enquirer" suggests. To quote from so recent a publication by a fellow townsman would have been to court detection. In Hurrion, Chatterton had all of Rowley's classical erudition and all of Rowley's theology (with the exception of one eminently Chattertonian sentiment) ready to hand. It remained for Chatterton to digest and to "antiquate" his materials. The process seems worth viewing at length.

In the following comparison, the whole of Rowley's *Sermon* is quoted by consecutive sections.[13]

Havynge whylomme ynn dyscourse provedd, orr soughte toe proove, the deitie of Chryste bie hys workes, names, and attributes, I shalle in nexte place seeke to proove the deeitie of Holye Spryte.

[Beginning of Sermon I.] Intending, if the Lord pleases, to *discourse* upon the Deity, Personality, Office, and *Works* of the Holy Spirit, I have chose the words now read, as a foundation of what I shall offer concerning the first of these, *the Deity of the Holy Ghost.* (3)

[Beginning of Sermon III.] *Having, in the preceding discourse, proved the Deity of* the Holy Ghost from his *names* and titles; I shall now proceed to some farther evidence of it, drawn from his *attributes.* (65)

Manne moste bee supplyedd wythe Holye Spryte toe have communyonn ryghtfullye of thynges whyche bee of Godde.

As he is the fountain of all wisdom, from whom we receive the holy scriptures, and a right understanding of them, we cannot see but by his light, nor know or acknowledge him, but by his assistance. (4)

Seyncte Paulle prayethe the Holye Spryte toe assyste hys flocke ynn these wordes, *The Holye Sprytes communyonn bee wythe you.*

[13] W. W. Skeat's text in *The Poetical Works of Thomas Chatterton* (London, 1905), II, 302–306. Pertinent passages from the first edition of Hurrion's six sermons on *The True Divinity of the Holy Spirit* are quoted beneath each section of Rowley, page numbers being given in parentheses. Nearly all of Chatterton's borrowings, it will be seen, come from three small parts of Hurrion's work (pp. 3–7, 11–14, and 114–125). Chatterton may merely have glanced beyond them.

he, is born, the Spirit is his forerunner; Christ

q Galat. vi. 8.　　r Rom. vi. 2, &c.

ʳ Γεννᾶται Χειϲὸς, πϱοϲέχει· βαπλίζελα μαϱλυϱεῖ. πϱο-
εϱχέϑει, ἀνάϱζη δυνάμεωϲ ϲπιϲελεῖ, συμπαϱεϱμαϱθέλ ἀνϱέϲ-
Χέϑα, διαϰλέχελαι· τι ʒ̓ δ̓ δύναλο τῆϲ τολμίαϲ μεγάλαν ϰ̀ το Θεόϲ;
ἐωϲ, πάλιν ἀ̓ϒεσημελάϲ ὁ Θεὸϲ ταϲϊϑπελελὰ λ̓ ϒεννί-
μμελ Χειϲοϲ πμϖϲα Χϱιϲϥ αϲϑϱοϰ σϱλ Χειϱα
ϲαϲϱοϰ πϱ τελεϲὶ λέϒελ ϰ δϒ λέγελαι· πνϵῦμα
τελεϲὶ πνϵῦμα Θεῶ λέγελαι —— πνεῦμα πϱϑϹϵⲩⲙⲓⲱ

Chatterton's Model and "Rowley's" Quotation from the Greek

As therefore *the apostle pray'd . . . to the Holy Spirit*, on the behalf of the Corinthians, that he would communicate of himself, to them, *in those words*, "The communion of the Holy Ghost be with you"; it is very proper to apply to him, for his gracious aid and assistance. (4)

Lette us dhere desyerr of hymm to ayde us, I ynne unplyteynge and you ynn understandynge hys deeite:

As the subject is very necessary, important, sublime, and difficult, I do not only *desire the prayers of my hearers, but also humbly invoke the assistance of him, concerning whom I am to speak,* that he may lead me into the truth, and *enable me to speak of him* the things that are right, and that may be to his glory, and our edification and comfort. (3–4)

lette us saye wythe Seyncte Cyprian, *Adesto, Sancte Spiritus, & paraclesin tuam expectantibus illabere cœlitus*; *sanctifica templum corporis nostri, & consecra inhabitaculum tuum*.

An example of this *we have in Cyprian*, that eminent servant of Christ, and martyr for him: When he composed his discourse concerning the Holy Spirit, he begun it with a solemn address to him; which being so agreeable to my present text and subject, it may not be improper to rehearse some part of it: "O Holy Spirit, be thou present; and from heaven shed down thy consolations on those that expect thee; sanctify the temple of our body, and consecrate it a habitation for thy self." [Hurrion quotes well beyond this point. A note supplies the Latin, with ascription to "Cyprian de Spiritu S. p. 484. b. 485.a. Ed. Pamelii."] (4–5)

Seyncte Paulle sayethe yee are the temple of Godde; forr the Spryte of Godde dwellethe ynn you. Gyff yee are the temple of Godde alleyne bie the dwellynge of the Spryte, wote yee notte that the Spryte ys Godde, ande playne proofe of the personne and glorye of the thryrde personne.

For *the apostle having said, that they were the temple of God*, as an explication and evidence of it, he added, in the very next sentence, *"The Spirit of God dwells in you"*, as in his temple, as it is explained in a following part of this epistle: *"Know you not* that your body is the temple of the Holy Ghost". (6)

If these things are consider'd, the allusion appears very beautiful; and the similitude between God's dwelling in the temple of old, and *the Holy Spirit's dwelling in believers*, as in his temple, is very apt and instructive, and carries in it *a striking conviction of the Deity, Personality and Glory of the Holy Ghost;* . . . (7)

The personne, gyftes, operatyonns, glorye, and deeitie, are all ynn Holye Spryte, as bee prooved fromm diffraunt textes of Scrypture: beeynge, as Seyncte Peter sayethe, of the same essentyall matterr as the Fadre ande Sonne, whoe are Goddes, the Holye Spryte moste undisputably bee Godde.

The word Spirit has *many significations in scripture,* of which I shall now take no notice; because it is not a spirit, or the spirit in general, but the Spirit of God in particular, of which my text speaks; which words often denote the Holy Ghost himself, *personally consider'd,* and not barely his *gifts* and *opperations;* which are often signified by the word Spirit: But here something is ascribed to him, which imports both *Deity* and *Personality,* as has, in part, been declared already, and may more fully afterwards. He is properly stiled, the Spirit of God; because he proceeds from God, and is of *the same nature and essence with the Father and Son,* who are God. *He is that Spirit which is of God by procession;* he is that Spirit which dwells in the saints, who are his temple; and *therefore he is himself God,* as has been already hinted. (11)

[Chatterton may well have read I *Peter* 1:2, 11–12. Hurrion's note to the last sentence above, citing John 15:26, would have sent him to the pages immediately following the epistles of Peter.]

The Spryte orr dyvyne will of Godde moovedd uponn the waterrs att the creatyonn of the worlde: thys meanethe the Deeitie.

I may add, that as the Holy Ghost is intended by the Spirit of God, in scripture, so mostly, if not always, when he is so called, there is something said of him, *which shews him to be that Spirit; which is also God:* As when it is said, *"the Spirit of God moved upon the waters, in the creation of the world."* (11–12)

I sayde, ynn mie laste discourse, the promyse of Chryste, whoe wythe Godde the Fadre wolde dwelle ynn the soughle of his decyples; howe coulde heie soe but bie myssyonn of Holye Spryte?

It signifies, that the Spirit himself is in believers. *Christ has promised* to the person that loves him, *that both he and the Father will come to him,* and make their abode with him. This is done *by the mission* and inhabitation *of the Holy Spirit.* (12)

Thys methynkethe prooveth ne alleyne the personallitie of Holye Spryte, but the verrie foundatyonne and grounde wurch of the Trinitie yttselfe.

Believers are an habitation of God, by or through the Spirit: For, as by the Spirit we have access to the Father, through the Son; so *it is by the Spirit, that both Father and Son come to, and dwell in the saints*; for he comes and takes his throne in the soul, as sent by the Father and Son. This informs us how the Father and Son are both said to dwell in the saints; and yet they are peculiarly the temples of the Holy Spirit, and he personally dwells in them . . . *by his immediate presence, and personal inhabitation,* he is in you, whom you have of God. (12–13)

The Holye Spryte cannot bee the goode thynges ande vyrtues of a manns mynde, sythence bie hymm wee bee toe fast keepe yese goode thynges: gyff wee bee toe keepe a vyrtue bie thatte vyrtue ytt selfe, meethynckes the custos bee notte fytted toe the charge. The Spryte orr Godde ys the auctoure of those goode thynges; and bie hys obeisaunce dheie mote alleyne bee helde.

It is likewise said, "That good thing that was committed to thee, keep by the Holy Ghost, which dwells in us." *Here is an evident distinction between the gifts and graces of the Spirit, and that Spirit who dwells in the saints.* If he dwelt in the saints only by his gifts and graces, then Paul's exhortation to Timothy, *to keep the good thing,* by the Holy Ghost which dwelt in him, had only signified this, *that he must keep those gifts and graces, by those gifts and graces which dwelt in him*: But if we take the latter clause of the personal indwelling of the Holy Spirit, the exhortation is plain and forceable, as the Holy Spirit *bestowed these good things* upon thee, and personally dwells in thee; so do thou look to him, to protect and preserve his own work. Besides, it appears, that the apostle speaks of the indwelling of the Spirit himself; because he applies it not only to Timothy, as had been proper, if his gifts and graces had been all that was meant by the indwelling of the Holy Spirit: But he says, which dwells in us; whereas Timothy's gifts and graces did not dwell in Paul, *but the Spirit, who is the* fountain and *author of them,* dwelt in Paul and Timothy both, and in all the saints; of him therefore it might be said, which dwelleth in us. (13–14)

I maie notte be doltysh ne hereticalle toe saie, whate wee calle consyence ys the hyltren warninge of the Spryte, to forsake our evylle waies before he dothe solely leave our steinedd soughles.

Appendix

[This seems the one entirely original sentence of the *Sermon*. It compares interestingly with a passage in Chatterton's short story *The Unfortunate Fathers* published in *The Town and Country Magazine* for January, 1770: "There is a principle in man (a shadow of the divinity) which constitutes him the image of God; you may call it conscience, grace, inspiration, the spirit, or whatever name your education gives it. If a man acts according to this regulator, he is right: if contrary to it, he is wrong." (Quoted in Myerstein, *Life*, p. 333.)]

Nete bee a greaterr proofe of mie argument thann the wurchys of Holye Spryte. The wurchys of Providence bee alleyne the wurchys of Godd, yette bee they the wurchys of the Spryte. Hee createdd manne, hee forslaggen hymm, hee agayne raysedd mann fromm the duste, ande havethe savedd all mankynde fromme eterne rewynn;

The works of preservation and *providence, are the works of the Holy Spirit, and proclaim him to be God*; seeing none else can perform them. (114)

The scriptures afford us numerous instances of his providential power and influence. *The conservation of the order and course of nature,* is ascribed to him in those words: "Thou sendest forth thy Spirit, they are created; thou renewest the face of the earth". The Holy Spirit is the immediate agent; *it is he that frustrates mens designs, and cuts off their lives* with his blast: "The grass withers, the flower fades, because the spirit of the Lord blows upon it". The surprizing deaths of Ananias and Saphira are memorable instances of this. (115)

To raise the dead requires the same power as at first created man; hence it is ascribed to God in scripture: "Why should it be thought an incredible thing with you, that God should raise the dead"? It might indeed be thought incredible, that any creature should do it: But cannot the same almighty power that form'd the body out of the dust at first, and breathed into it the breath of life, *raise it out of the dust* a second time, and reinfuse the same vital Spirit? (117)

he raysedd Chryste fromme the deade, hee made the worlde, and hee shalle destroye ytt.

Christ's resurrection was a kind of second creation; therefore it is spoke of as a begetting or new making of him: "Thou art my Son, this day have I begotten thee"; *explain'd of Christ's resurrection; which was spoke when he was raised from the dead.* (117)

He [the Holy Spirit] imparts his gifts and influences as he will. He seems to be addressed, as the North-wind, to blow upon the church, to blast her corruptions, and purify her members; *for he is a Spirit of judgment, and of burning* . . . (147)

[Chatterton may well have taken *judgment and burning* in the last quotation as a reference to the Day of Judgment and the destruction of the world. Hurrion suggests that the Holy Spirit "made the worlde" in his application of *Genesis* 1:2 quoted above, p. 184, but the idea recurs frequently in his pages.]

Gyff the Spryte bee notte Godde, howe bee ytt the posessynge of the Spryte dothe make a manne sayedd toe bee borne of Godde? Ytt requyreth the powerr of Godde toe make a manne a new creatyonn, yette suche dothe the Spryte.

Believers are born of the Spirit, quickened and renewed by the Holy Ghost: *This is a new creation, and requires the same almighty power, to effect, as the first creation did.* . . . If the Spirit is not God by nature, but is a creature, *how are they said to be born of God, who are regenerated by the Spirit?* (119)

Thus sayethe Seynte Gregorie Naz. of the Spryte and hys Wurchys:

[The fragmentary *Sermon* terminates with the passage in Greek which is reproduced as Chatterton inscribed it in the illustration opposite page 181.]

I shall therefore only add a more general account of him, and his divine works, as I find them represented by one of the ancients, and so conclude the doctrinal part of this branch of my subject. "Christ, says he, is born, the Spirit is his forerunner; Christ is baptized, he bears his testimony; Christ is tempted, he heads him away; Christ works miracles, he is with him; Christ ascends . . . [Hurrion quotes well beyond this point. He gives the Greek text in a note and cites his source as "Gregor. Nazianz. Orat. 3. p. 610, 611. Ed. Par." See the illustration opposite page 181.]

3

If this comparison does not show Chatterton at his full stature as a poet, it at least reveals him as much more than an indiscriminate magpie. The ideas and often the words are Hurrion's, but the voice is of the "goode preeste Rowlie." Thanks to Browning's habit of random reading, we have at last a satisfactory answer to a very old puzzle.

INDEX

INDEX

191